NATURE, NURTURE
and
NOSTALGIA

NATURE, NURTURE
and
NOSTALGIA

(Gleaned from the BLACK RIVER JOURNAL)

by

LOUIS MIHALYI

Artwork by
JOHN NORTON

Published by
North Country Books, Inc.
Utica, New York

DEDICATION

To Bernice, my helpmate and wife, who is my severest and most gentle critic, who corrects my spelling, who monitors my grammar, who guides me when I get off the path and who laughs at my jokes.

January 1985
Louis Mihalyi
Glenfield, NY 13343

Table of Contents

CHAPTER 1

RUFFED GROUSE

©1984 JOHN NORTON

Ruffed Grouse
Woods Drummer

He is known by dozens of names, ruffed grouse, partridge, drumming grouse, patridge. Hunters know him as a wily, wary bird.

In colonial times he was known as the "fool hen". Records show that the colonists made considerable use of the bird as food, to the extent that servants complained because the bird was served so frequently. So tame and unsuspecting, grouse could be harvested simply by knocking them off the branches with sticks or stones. This is not the picture the present day grouse hunter will give you. This is an excellent example of adaptation. Only the wariest of birds survived to reproduce and in just one or two hundred years an entirely different bird evolved.

Our north country partridge is a beautiful stately bird, bantam in size and featuring a broad tail. There are two phases,

1

red and brown. The ruff, a band of dark feathers on the neck from which it gets its name, is expanded to form a sort of collar giving the bird a regal appearance. The average fall weight is somewhat larger than one and a half pounds for the male, several ounces less for the female.

The ruffed grouse is basically a ground bird feeding on insects and seeds. However, he can and does spend considerable time in trees especially in winter when he feeds off the buds of popple, apple and other hardwoods. The preferred habitat seems to be a mixed cover, second growth hardwood with patches of alder, popple, birch. Broken woodlands with plenty of edges along farm lands produce plenty of birds.

The nest is always on or near the ground. It may be in a hollow next to a stump, under a log or in a thicket. It is constructed of whatever is at hand which will blend with the background, twigs, leaves, grass, weeds and a few old feathers. It is so inconspicuous and the hen so bland that she can hardly be seen as she incubates her dozen or so eggs. She will stay on the nest until the last moment when under other conditions she would be long gone.

Popping Sound

Sometimes while in the woods one will hear a distant pop-pop-popping like a starting gas engine. This is the sound of the drumming grouse. Drumming is confined to males and is most frequent in the spring, climaxing in May. Although it may be heard occasionally throughout the year, it is thought to be part of the courting ritual. The male mounts a log, boulder, stump, rock outcropping or even a snow drift and proceeds to beat the air with his wings. This rapid beating of the curved wings produces a hollow popping sound that may carry a mile and is thought to charm the shy hen and perhaps bring the two together. The drumming is also thought to be a territorial sign, warning other males of impending combat if trespass is not avoided.

During the fall the young of the season undergo a curious wildness, the so-called "crazy-flight". They fly recklessly and with abandon, seemingly attempting to go through rather than around.

Dead birds are often found at this time of the year having flown blindly into windows or against buildings. I once returned from a partridge hunting trip with two birds and not having had to fire a shot. One bird tried to fly through a woven wire fence

2

and a few steps farther on another crashed into the side of an abandoned barn. It would appear that this crazy flying is a dispersal technique whereby the summer brood, now mature, seeks new territory.

When the proper snow and weather conditions are present the ruffed grouse will engage in what is known as "snow roosting." The bird will dive from a perch or directly from flight into a bank of loose snow. Well into the snow bank a hollow is created and the bird remains snug and warm while the storm rages overhead. From the droppings left behind it has been determined that birds may remain several days snug and safe from the elements.

This magnificent bird is truly representative of our North Country. It survives our adversities with aplomb. It prevails. It is my candidate for state bird.

CHAPTER 2

Horseradish
Liquid Fire

Today I dug some horseradish and had some for lunch. I was so eager for the taste that I ended the meal munching crackers spread with the freshly ground herb.

If you have a square yard of garden tucked back where it is out of the way you can have your own supply of this pungent weed. It belongs to the mustard family and comes to us from Europe. As with most plants, a rich loam is preferable for the growing medium. It should be loose so that root growth will not be inhibited. Obtain a few small roots from a friend or order them from your nursery catalog. From a piece four to six inches long make several lengthwise slices about ½ inch thick. Plant these LARGE END UP about a foot apart with the large end about an inch or so under the soil. These roots are conical so there should be no trouble determining the large end, but be sure that it is up.

Some time in June or July, as your fancy dictates, lift your now sturdy roots. Remove the soil from around the top of the main root leaving the lower part undisturbed. Carefully cut off all the side roots leaving the main root intact. This will force the main stem to grow in size making preparation for the table much simpler. Recover the pruned root. You might use some new compost to replace the original soil. Water, sit back and wait until fall, October or later if you can stand it. Harvest your winter's supply, leaving the rest for spring.

If all has gone well, you should have several nice large roots to work with. These should be peeled and ground. We used to use the hand meat grinder until my wife discovered that the blender with a little water saved copious tears and smarting nostrils. Pack the results in jars and store in the refrigerator. Try packing some in white vinegar. Plain or with cream this makes a nice change. Try adding some to your pickles. Horseradish-dill makes a combination that is hard to beat.

In the spring you can again make a harvest, preparing

4

enough to last the summer. Be sure that you save a few roots to replant. Usually one growing season will give usable roots. After two or more growing seasons the roots will be of excellent size, ideal for harvesting.

While in Japan in the Army of Occupation, I was invited to a Japanese banquet. We were seated on the floor at a long, low table. The sides of the house were open so that the villagers could watch from the darkness outside. Flanking each guest was an attendant who knelt attentively on her knees. Her main duties, as I saw it, were to keep the cups, glasses, plates and bowls filled. You could never get your tea just right for whenever you took a swallow, she poured more into the cup.

In front of me was a shallow dish containing several substances flanked by some jars which I found out later were various sauces. All of which were to be used by each guest to make a dip to suit his tastes. Among the items on the flat dish was a small pellet about the size of a robin's egg. It looked interesting and to show my dexterity with the chopsticks, I popped it into my mouth.

My attendant gave a little gasp and put her hand to her face. Then she chattered something to the next attendant down the line who looked at me with widening eyes. Well, you guessed it — it was horseradish, freshly ground horseradish. I don't know whether it was an especially virulent oriental variety or whether I had become less tolerant to it, not having had horseradish for three or four years, but it was potent.

It hit my nose almost as soon as it hit my taste buds. My nose twitched, it smarted, it throbbed. It seemed to contort itself across my face like a dog rolling to avoid a swarm of yellow jackets. My eyes blurred, they watered, they crossed, they popped and went in and out of focus. My ears rang, then pounded, bells clanged and cymbals clashed and I'm sure my scalp rose up off my skull. An inept Indian could have taken it without using a knife.

With all the dignity and decorum I could muster, I reached for the tea cup which had just been refilled. I sloshed its scalding contents down my throat. Through unseeing eyes I looked in the direction of my attendant, managed a weak smile and nodded as though to indicate that the sample was good.

When I finally recovered I thought I noticed a modicum of increased respect, or was it awe, from my little attendant. Two more pellets appeared in my condiment dish and an air of expectancy seemed to pervade my side of the table.

5

CHAPTER 3

JOHN NORTON

Worm Harvest
The Fine Art of Nightcrawling

Nightcrawling does not refer to the inebriate making his way home from the local pub at 1:30 in the morning. Night-crawling refers to the process of harvesting earthworms that are highly desirable for use in the fine art of angling. There are more than three thousand species of earthworms in the world, ranging from the very tiny to a six foot native of Australia. We are most interested here in Lumbrivus terrestrus, the common ten inch variety.

To understand the technique of gathering earthworms, one should have an understanding of the beast itself. Earthworms are segmented worms with our subject having about one hundred fifty segments. Within each segment is a circular muscle. Four pairs of tiny bristles called setae project from the bottom and sides of each segment.

The anterior, or head, or perhaps more appropriately the front end of the organism (since it does not have much of a head on its shoulders), has a mouth and not much more. There is a concentration of enlarged nerve centers that passes for a brain. There are no sense organs, but there are specialized nerve cells that are sensitive to light and sound.

When light falls on these light sensitive cells the worms become uncomfortable and withdraw to their darker burrows.

There appears to be a greater concentration of these light sensitive cells at the anterior end than in other parts of the body. This front end is much darker than the tail.

About a third of the way back is a swelling called the clitellum. This structure is involved in reproduction, which is of interest to the worm hunter since it is the reproductive drive that brings the worms to the surface after a rain. Earthworms are hermaphroditic. That is, each worm contains organs that produce both eggs and sperm. Worms exchange sperm above the surface of the soil. Each then lays its own fertilized eggs.

Retreat

When the worm emerges on the surface, it does not immediately leave its burrow. It searches for another worm within the radius of its body length. The rear portion remains within the burrow entrance. The setae are projected outward and wedge tightly against the sides of the burrow. This very firmly anchors the worm, giving it something to pull against should it retreat. If the worm finds another nearby, they align themselves and exchange sperm which is stored for later use.

The last thing that the hunter should know about is the powerful longitudinal muscles which run from head to tail. Pound for pound, the earthworm is stronger than a man. When an anchored earthworm decides to go home, its withdrawal is almost instantaneous.

The basic equipment you will need as an earthworm hunter is a flashlight, a small pail to hold your catch, and a strong back. These items together with the proper technique will get you worms.

But there are some modifications that can make things easier. I like to use one of those lights that strap to your head with the beam shining down from your forehead. Some claim that a red light is less detectable by the worms. I have tried it by covering the lens with red cellophane but find that the reduced intensity hinders me more than it helps. Perhaps you may find it useful.

The battery is attached to my belt or put in a back pocket, with the cord running under my jacket to my head. Attached to my belt is a small pail. Within the pail is a smaller tin can containing sawdust. This I use to clean and dry my hands after handling several worms. The mucus that covers the worm's body is very slippery. Once the fingers become covered with mucus, gripping the worms becomes difficult, with considerable hazard to the worms.

I have a minor problem with this setup, brought about by my need for trifocal glasses. When a worm is located in the light beam, I bend lower to grasp it. To use the close-up lens, I must tilt my head, thus moving the beam away from the worm. It takes several adjustments to get things right.

Now you scan the ground until you spot a worm, having waited, after a soaking rain, until it is quite dark. The lighter end, the posterior or rear is securely lodged within the burrow. Because the worms are so fast, you need to give yourself every advantage. So make your grab for the lighter end. The withdrawing worm will have to move through your fingers giving you a slight edge.

Technique

Once you have a grip on the worm, slowly pull it out of its burrow. It is surprising the tenacity these animals exhibit. But since it is stonger than a man it is quite understandable. After a few moments of steady pulling the worm will tire. After all, you are bigger and should have a little more staying power. If you are careful, you will drop a whole, undamaged worm into your pail.

Since your pail is on your belt and the light on your head, you have both hands free to harvest. I must admit that because of a certain amount of senility that has encroached on my life, that I do not use two hands. I use one arm to rest on a knee, the other to engage in hunting. This eases my back which at times seems to be more senile than the rest of me. As the arms tire, I switch. However, if you are younger and more agile you may be able to use both hands simultaneously. I once watched a young woman, in a patch loaded with worms, alternately use each hand to pour a continuous stream of worms into her pail.

The front end is more sensitive to light. So once a worm is spotted, move the beam of your light off to one side, keeping the worm within sight but in dim light. Lumbricus, being sensitive to sound, particularly ground vibrations, requires that you move slowly and carefully. Any slight vibration will cause them to pop back into their burrows. Reworking the area after a rest period is usually productive.

Whether you are a nightcrawler for fun or profit (worms in this area bring five cents and up each) you can enhance your efforts with a little knowledge and some simple equipment. So, understand your worm, equip yourself (including a bottle of linament) and have fun.

8

CHAPTER 4

Parasites
We All Have 'em

Great fleas have little fleas
On their backs to bite 'em
And little fleas have lesser fleas
And so ad infinitum

—Agustus Morgan 1806-1871

Although Morgan wrote this doggerel over 100 years ago its truth becomes more apparent with each passing day. Just about everything has its parasite. You name it and if it is alive it will probably be carrying some excess baggage in the form of a parasite.

Although we like to think of ourselves as a cut above most living things, humans are no exceptions. Among our more visible parasites are fleas, lice and ticks. Mosquitoes, horse flies, deer flies, black flies and other biting insects feed on us when we expose areas of succulent flesh.

We may be infected with round worms, tape worms and flukes. The older you get the more likely you are to have the eyebrow bug. This is a tiny species of life that inhabits only the pores of the human eyebrow. It rarely causes any harm. It is not much of a parasite but nevertheless it qualifies in Morgan's view. Most of us who host this parasite never even realize it.

All animals, directly or indirectly, are parasitic on plants. The most obvious plant parasites are, of course, insects. All kinds of chewing and sucking insects attack our plants. The gardener, the farmer, continually battle insect parasitism.

We are learning to battle some of these parasites with their own parasites. The various cabbage eating worms can be easily controlled by innoculation with a bacterium (Bacillus thuringiensis). This parasite is harmless to humans but creates a disease in the larva which causes their death, interrupting the reproductive cycle.

The Japanese beetle can now be similarly controlled with a beetle disease that causes its death but does not effect the birds and other animals that feed on the insect. These are fine examples of biological control wherein a controlling agent is used that effects only the desired parasite and is non-toxic to other life forms in the environment. These agents are now readily available from the various seed firms or your local seed store or nursery. Many plants are attacked by rusts, smuts, mildews and other fungal parasites. We have to watch continually for their attacks.

If it is alive, it will be a host. Perhaps the ultimate parasite for all other life forms is the bacteria. Bacteria infect most animal and plant forms in some manner. But what about bacteria? Are they classed as living things? Do they have parasites as Morgan implies? They certainly do. There is a large group of viruses called bacteriophages that attack and destroy bacteria. These forms, which are the subject of considerable controversy as to whether or not they are living organisms, are perhaps the supreme parasites.

And so, Agustus, perhaps you saw more clearly than you knew. Every living thing has its parasite. The parasites have their parasites and so ad infinitum.

CHAPTER 5

Garden Journal
A Helpful Tool

I forget. This tendency increases with age. Things that I vow to remember to infinity are promptly forgotten. Thus I come to one of the most useful of my gardening aids, the garden journal. A journal is more than a diary. In addition to day to day events, it records ideas, reflections, experiences, day dreams and numerous notes to myself.

I first started keeping my garden records in 1956. Previous to that I had made notes on returned order blanks, on the pages of seed catalogs and scraps of paper. These of course were promptly misplaced, scattered around the house and were of little use.

A cloth bound accountant's journal became the document. Each year a map of the garden is drawn. The location of each vegetable is plotted. Its name, the source of seed, date planted and date of germination are recorded in place. Then follows a chronology of first harvests, total harvest, insect problems, diseases, transplanting data, weather, last frost, first frost, fertilizers used, rainfall, watering schedules and anything else pertinent to my garden. Separate maps are kept showing the location of fruit and nut trees, names, sources, and dates planted.

The successful garden requires rotation. Corn culture is a good example. It is a heavy feeder and despite what I feel should be ample fertilization it nevertheless tends to exhaust the soil. So it should be planted in a different area each year in so far as is possible. About a quarter of my garden is devoted to corn. Thanks to my garden journal as a memory aid I have what amounts to a four year corn rotation.

Cycles

Other vegetables have similar cycles but since they are not planted in such quantity the problem is not quite as acute.

However, I am very careful to insure that the tomatoes do not get around to the same place more often than every five or six years. Similar rotations involve all the other crops I grow. Soil depletion, insects and disease dictate my schedules.

My chronology, kept through the summer and fall, will include admonitions to plant the jumbo cabbage farther apart, plant fewer zucchini, start the peppers and egg plant earlier, a variety of do's and don'ts. The new varieties that I am trying will receive detailed planting as well as performance data. Evaluation and the decision to include the item in next year's garden may be made on the spot or may wait until the winter months when I am ensconced with my seed catalogs.

The journal is a great help when I am making out my seed orders. I cannot remember how Victory cucumbers compared with Princess. The journal points out that Victory was inferior. So we will go with Princess and try another variety with it.

Sometime in the fall when the garden is nearly put to bed for the winter, perhaps during a respite while finishing the compost pile, I sit down and write a review of the season. This may be only a paragraph or may run to a page or two. I notice that these reviews get longer with each passing year. During the winter I read these histories with relish. I can recall the delicious (delicious is every sense of the word) incidents. The first radish, crisp but tender, the early corn, the sandwich of Ithaca lettuce wrapped around a freshly pulled baby Pioneer carrot, the sweet juice of a sun ripened tomato. Failures are recorded, of course. I may not recall them with gladness but their evidence on the page helps to avoid future misadventures.

Clippings

Magazine and newspaper clippings embellish my journal. Gardening pamphlets are securely fastened so they will not wander. One section is graced by an assortment of rare tropical flowers that would never grow in the area but which a small assistant, using her scissors and paste many years ago, thought would give my journal color.

My journal looks worn. The cloth cover is becoming threadbare and needs repair. It is discolored and dirty from fertilizer spills, sudden showers, small dogs and tiny human footprints and of course my earth-stained fingers. An unknowing person would consign it to the trash after handling it carefully to avoid contamination. But to me it is a treasure. It is a guide for future endeavors. It is a memory aid, a means of recalling and enjoying the gardens of my past.

If there is one thing wrong with my journal keeping, it is that I don't write enough. I should make a habit of writing something in it each day. Too frequently I put off recording something until another day to find that is has escaped for all time.

I strongly recommend that you keep a journal even though you may only have a few house plants or a row of lettuce.

CHAPTER 6

Chickadee
Mr. Congeniality

Just about every bird feeder has its share of chickadees. This is fortunate since these birds are among the most friendly, most interesting and most easily observed of our bird friends.

Because of their friendliness and curiosity they are easily tamed and will after a very few tries easily come to feed out of one's hand. Every jacket, every coat I own has a supply of sunflower seeds in a pocket so that whenever I'm outside and knowledgeable chickadees are present, I can feed them. Sometimes as I move through my woods, a cloud of these little balls of fluff will follow me around.

Known as the common, eastern or blackcapped chickadee, our north country chickadee is slightly over five inches in length. It is the only small bird that has a black bib in front with a black cape and white cheeks. Because of its small size there is a high surface to volume ratio. This means that there is proportionally greater heat loss than with larger birds. This little engine runs at a high temperature and at a high rate of speed. The heart rate is five hundred beats per minute at rest and double that with high activity. For its size, its food requirements are enormous.

The minute I open my garage door in the morning, particularly in winter, the chickadees come to be fed. There seems to be a sort of hierarchy, a pecking order. Some birds (probably the young of the current year) will always wait until the others have fed. Among the older birds there is also a definite order. Each seems to defer to those above it.

I have not been able to determine the precise order. A dominant bird will posture when a lesser bird lights simultaneously on my hand. With tiny beaks opened they make what are apparently very frightening gestures. The others, intimidated and thus preempted, will back off to wait until the captain has fed before moving to take their seeds.

Woodpecker Holes

The nests are usually located in old woodpecker holes or similar natural cavities. I've rarely been successful in getting them to nest in my birdhouses. The nests are neat, tiny structures lined with grasses, fur and small feathers. Four to eight spotted white eggs comprise the usual clutch.

The chickadee's song is his name and thus easily identified. There is a second song which I usually hear beginning in late winter. This is a very beautiful two or three note affair that is very similar to the Phoebe. Reports of phoebes in late February or early March are probably not phoebes but chickadees welcoming the longer and warmer days.

On cold nights I wonder how my chickadees are doing. I worry about their making it through the night. I am always grateful that a miracle has been performed when they reappear each morning. To survive the intense cold they squirrel themselves in a well sheltered nook and fluff up their feathers. I have seen them hunker down in my wood pile but usually they seem to go to a nearby swamp where the wind is minimal.

I've tried different modes of feeding them other than from my hand. Within a short time they will take sunflower seeds from my lips. At first they hover, picking a seed in flight. But after a while, they perch on my chin and take their time in selecting a seed as we eye each other at close range. Sometimes they will look expectantly into a jacket pocket. When they light on my hand or chin I can feel their cold feet. Some are much colder than others. Translating my human experience into bird experience, I infer that these are females.

One time I was sitting in a reclining chair under a tree in late autumn. The chickadees were about. I placed a handful of sunflower seeds on my chest and watched their antics at close hand. The sun was warm. It was a pleasant day and I soon fell asleep. The supply of seeds was shortly exhausted and the birds frustrated. I was sharply awakened when one educated bird perched on my ear and shouted into the ear canal. I don't know where or how he learned his anatomy, but it was effective. The translated call, "Is anybody in there? We're out of food", brought me back and a resupply of seed was assured.

The chickadee is a fun bird. Make his acquaintance. Become his friend. He will give you much pleasure and return your friendship.

CHAPTER 7

Blackberries
August Treasure

It looks like a good year for blackberries. The canes are loaded with their white blossoms. The air is perfumed with their scent. Of course, I said the same thing last year and then the dry weather in August produced nothing but nubbins. I have a few blackberry bushes in my woods which I pick for the occasional dessert. It is also a nice place to be able to go to in the morning for a few handfuls for the breakfast cereal.

Some years ago I was keeping watch on a patch not far from the house, waiting for them to reach their peak. On the day I went to pick them, there were no ripe berries. I found only the light cores where the ripe berries had been. There were no ripe berries on the ground so someone or something had beaten me to the harvest. The same thing occurred a few days later in another small patch. All the ripe berries had been harvested.

So I took my container and went farther back into the woods. I found an unmolested patch and soon was filling my pail. It was then that I discovered the culprit. I had been stabbed in the back.

At the time we had a nice dog, part collie, part dog and part other dog. He was a gentle animal who watched over our off-spring as though they were his own. As I picked he was also picking. He would approach a drooping cluster and lick off the ripe berries. Only those that were dead ripe, easily dislodged and perfect in flavor went into his mouth. The thorns on the canes lacerated his tongue and after a few minutes he was bleeding profusely. It didn't seem to bother him and he picked until we left for home.

Pine Lake

The most beautiful berries I ever found were up near Pine Lake. During a summer vacation when I was in high school, a good friend and I were camping not too far from the lake. We found a patch of berries in what was called the "chip yard." This was a large area where in the past pulp had been peeled and sawed. This left a large space covered with bark, sawdust and chips, an ideal place for blackberries.

It was almost a jungle. The canes were well above our heads. We picked with our hands above our shoulders. Oh, what berries, big, flat, shining black, they were as large as your thumb. Bursting with juice, as many went into my mouth as went into my pail.

We entered the patch and were soon lost from one another. I soon filled my pail and called to my partner but received no answer. I could hear him from time to time picking in front of me but could not seem to make him hear. This area had at one time been a magnificent forest of pine. Logging and particularly fire had decimated the woodland. All over were large fire-charred stumps.

Not getting any response to my calls, I climbed one of the stumps to get above the jungle and try to see what was going on. At this time my partner, a blackberry connoisseur, a black bear, also climbed a stump. We both stared at each other over the tangle of berry canes. We both backed down from our perches in haste. We both fled the berry patch in opposite directions. We both set record times for the distances involved. Each was probably equally fearful of the other.

Large Harvest

After the excitement had died down it was decided that we should reap a large harvest. The berries were so unusual that we wanted to share them with our parents. The only container we had that was large enough was my packbasket. It was large, sturdy and would hold many quarts. The berries were so plentiful and huge that we had the basket filled in no time.

The hike to camp was a mile or two. The ride out to civilization was 12 to 14 miles over bumpy roads in an ancient model T Ford. I tried to protect the basket, but by the time we arrived home the contents had shrunk to about a quarter of the volume of the packbasket. Most of those huge succulent fruits were reduced to mush and juice. My basket remained stained and smelled of blackberries for many years.

Blackberries are at their best dead ripe and sun-warm right off the bush. The flavor of the fresh ripe berry is incomparable.

18

The next best is with cream and sugar or on cereal. They make a fine addition to a fruit salad. There is nothing quite like a warm, fresh out of the oven, blackberry pie. They are great in muffins. They can be canned but are better frozen. Drying used to be popular. And then there is blackberry wine.

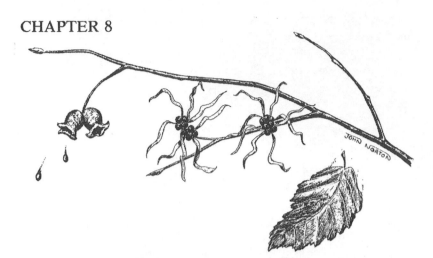

CHAPTER 8

Witch Hazel
Winter Bloomers

A curious shrub that grows in our North Country is the witch hazel, sometimes called winterbloom or snapping hazel nut. It is curious for several reasons. The one that appeals to me is its habit of blooming in the fall or winter.

Well after its leaves have dropped, in late September, October or November, pretty yellow flowers appear. It is a glorious sight in late autumn, when one does not expect new blossoms, to come upon a witch hazel in full bloom. Not that the shrub is all that spectacular but for the time of year it is endearing. It is this late blooming aspect that gives it the common name of winterbloom.

These flowers, which appear in clusters at the joints of twigs are far from being spectacular as individuals. They consist of four ribbon-like lemon yellow petals. The petals hang down and twist around. They seem to have no set permanent place or formal pattern as does the tulip petal. But numbers of these blossoms when viewed together on a shrub during a November snow storm make a spectacular bouquet.

A second, curious aspect is its method of seed dispersal. The seeds, dark, black ovals are encased in a capsule that ripens with the cold. When fully ripe and dry, the capsule opens and vigorously expels the seeds. These may fly up to ten feet away. This gives rise to the name snapping hazel nut. This dispersal technique is not limited to the witch hazel but is unique for the time of year it occurs.

The witch hazel (Haamamelis Virginiana) has an oval to heart-shaped leaf. Its margins are irregular and wavy toothed. The length varies from two to six inches. The leaf undersides are densely covered with rusty hairs.

The plant ranges from New England to Florida and west to the Mississippi. In the northern reaches of its range it is most likely to be a shrub with several stems. But in the southern portions of its range it may become a tree 30 feet high with a trunk reaching 12 inches in diameter.

Both the leaves and an extract of witch hazel bark were valued additions to our grandparent's medicine chest. Largely used to assuage burns and inflamation, it can still be found in medicine cabinets and on drug store shelves. It seems to have value in promoting healing. Its value for reducing swellings and relieving pain was well known by the American Indian. The witch hazel that we see today on the druggist's shelf is probably an extract of bark in an alcohol solution. It is useful in treating insect bites.

My grandmother always had a small bottle of witch hazel which she used on all my burns, cuts and scrapes.

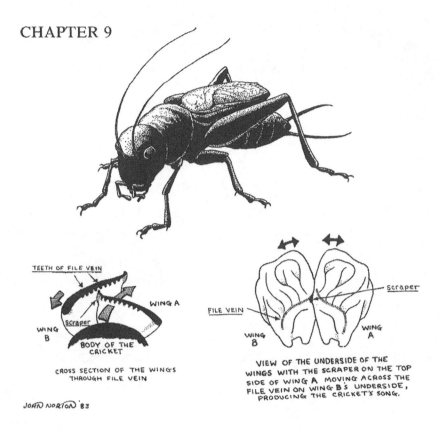

CHAPTER 9

TEETH OF FILE VEIN

WING A

WING B

scraper

BODY OF THE CRICKET

CROSS SECTION OF THE WINGS THROUGH FILE VEIN

scraper

FILE VEIN

WING B

WING A

VIEW OF THE UNDERSIDE OF THE WINGS WITH THE SCRAPER ON THE TOP SIDE OF WING A MOVING ACROSS THE FILE VEIN ON WING B'S UNDERSIDE, PRODUCING THE CRICKET'S SONG.

JOHN NORTON '83

Crickets
Late Summer Songster

Some time around the end of May or certainly the first part of June I will hear the first cricket of the season. I don't usually look for it but suddenly it is there and I am glad. The sound of crickets on a warm summer evening has a soothing sound for me. I guess this goes back to my youth when I would listen to a cricket behind the mopboard in my bedroom as I fell asleep.

There are a large number of crickets and cricket-like animals. I don't pretend to be able to identify the varieties. My crickets are large, fat and shiny black. While they do not fly, they do possess wings. The wings on the male are larger than those of the female. The best way to tell the sexes apart is by the ovipositer or egg-laying tube that protrudes well behind the female.

Crickets do not travel very much. This is particularly true for the male. He establishes a territory and pretty much stays there. Encroaching males are confronted and soon driven away. In this way, with each defending his territory, the males become spaced out over any given area. Once ensconced on his homestead, the male does not travel far. He stays at home and sings, waiting for the female to come to him.

The singing is done with the wings. The front wings of the male feature a file-like structure which is rubbed over a toughened scraper on the opposite rear wing. This creates a vibration which is amplified by the wing surface and the cricket song is air born. Most crickets are right-handed or more appropriately "right-winged." That is, they rub the right fore wing over the left rear wing when they sing. As with any population where there is "handedness", there are a few "left-wingers." The object of this singing, of course, is to attract a mate. The song says in very plain cricket, "Attractive lonesome male, desirous of establishing a relationship with attractive female. Object matrimony." A female ready to mate, hearing the siren song will go to the loudest male, which is probably the nearest. This is one time when loudness might be considered as synonymous with amorous.

Temperature effects the rate of the cricket chirp. The warmer it is the faster come the chirps. There have been several formulas devised whereby one can reasonably determine the current temperature. One of the simplest is count the number of chirps in thirteen seconds, add forty and you will get the Fahrenheit temperature. It should be noted that different species will give somewhat different results.

Crickets are largely vegetarian, consuming mostly dead plant material. They are no threat to your garden. When in the house they might chew a little on a curtain. But by and large they are not considered pests. In some Far Eastern countries they are kept in cages for their singing abilities. While I have not gone to that extent, I do favor their song. I take great pleasure in a cricket concert in the cool of the evening.

The sharp chirp of the crickets tell me that life is going on, that one of nature's cycles is fulfilling itself. Nature is replete with cycles. Whether we like it or not we are a part of this intricate tangle. We are a part of many cycles and knowingly or unknowingly we affect many others. We all should be aware of this. We all should try to minimize our intrusions.

CHAPTER 10

Cleaning Bookshelves
You Have to Stand by Old Friends

I hate to discard books. I just keep accumulating them. My bookshelves gradually become crammed. Every nook and cranny gets stuffed with volumes, pamphlets and tomes that I can't let go.

The other day my gentle wife suggested that I go through one of the shelves and try to get rid of some of the excess. So, I sat down one afternoon to do a real clean-up job. The first thing I noticed was Taylor's "Encyclopedia of Gardening", two volumes. One of these could be discarded or given away. But then it might be nice to have one upstairs for perusing when I dream with the seed catalogs during the long cold winter months. The other could be useful down in the cellar where I do my indoor gardening under the lights. So perhaps I should keep both copies.

"Five Acres and Independence", a dog-eared paperback, an armed forces edition, slim, narrow cut to fit the pocket of a fatigue jacket. An old friend, its inspired dreams kept me going during those days long ago in the Pacific. Here is one that won't go. It is too much a part of me.

"Success With Small Fruits" by E. P. Roe, 1881. I have the 1886 edition. The varieties he talks about are out of date but much of what he says still holds. Chapter XXXII is entitled, "A Few Rules and Maxims". Rule No. 1 says, "Never put off til spring work that might be done in the fall. Spring is always too short for the labor it brings, even when not wet and late." So he had those problems, too.

His rules are all pretty good. You would think they came from the typewriter of some modern author. Rule No. 14 — "Mulch everything you can. Save all the leaves and litter that can be gathered in one place, and apply it around the plants only when the ground is moist. Dry ground covered with mulch may be kept dry all summer." Sound advice even if nearly a hundred years old. No, I can't let this one go.

Here is a book on managing a greenhouse. I've always wanted a greenhouse, one attached to the house. I used to dream about it. When we built our home I could not see the expense and settled on a "greenporch." Enclosed and heated it gave me a little greenhouse feeling. Now with fuel so costly I'm afraid I'll never get a true greenhouse. But I have my dreams and this book has inspired many of them. I guess I'll just keep it.

Next is a bundle of pamphlets, from a Department of Agriculture bulletin on building log structures dated 1931 to blueberry culture and beekeeping. Thirty eight in all, most of which I've never actually used but all of which I have perused. I might have need of one of them in the future.

A book on gardening under lights, poorly written, full of not much, yet it did have several good ideas for suspending and arranging lights. I plan to try one of them next year and will need the book for reference.

Another book on indoor gardening, not much, but does have some good photographs especially of several plant species I no longer have and a number that I think I'd like to try.

"How to Cook Wild Game". This one uses a lot of soda, but does have a good recipe for stuffing wild duck. I remember the first time we tried it some twenty five years ago. Those ducks were mighty good.

Here is a dandy little volume. "128 House Plants You Can Grow", by Rob Herwig. This is one I have to keep. It is well illustrated and has nice little picture symbols that even I can understand. I've checked off those species that I've grown at one time or another. A majority are checked. No, this one stays.

Here are several "How to . . ." books. I always like to look at these even if I'm not interested in caning a chair or hooking a rug. But then, some time I might.

Well, there I've spent a pleasant afternoon. I've renewed some old friendships, redreamed some old dreams. The shelf is all in order, nice and neat. The books are nicely rearranged and I didn't throw out a single thing.

CHAPTER 11

Shrike
Bad Guy? Not at All

Sometimes called "Butcher Bird," the Northern Shrike has a somewhat dubious reputation. Its appearance causes consternation among small birds and birdfeeder proprietors alike. The shrikes are classified as songbirds because of the sometimes melodious notes that it sings in early spring. Sometimes these are reminiscent of the catbird. As the name butcher bird implies, these are songbirds of prey.

Their food consists largely of insects together with small birds and mammals and an occasional frog or small snake. A peculiarity of these animals, and apparently limited to them, is their habit of impaling their catch on thorns. Whether this is a storage process or an aid in holding the catch for consumption is not certain.

Many years ago, while hunting cottontail rabbits in a thorn apple pasture, I came upon a tree that was decorated with three mice neatly skewered on individual thorns. I was unfamiliar with the shrike at the time and thus was severely puzzled with this phenomenon. It was not until some years later that I knew what had happened. This past fall I was shown a mouse neatly cached in the crotch of a small bush. Alerted, I spied a shrike a few days later.

The Northern Shrike is a robin-sized bird about 10 inches long. It is bluish black on top with white below. The wings and tail are black. A conspicuous black cheek mask running through the eye to the bill is a good identification mark. Its flight is described as "heavy."

If you see a robin-sized bird drop low from its high perch of advantage, continue in a somewhat labored fashion a few feet above the ground only to suddenly glide upward to another high perch, you are probably looking at a Northern Shrike.

This flight characteristic is a good preliminary identification mark. A very distinctive feature is the strongly hooked beak. It is the only North Country song bird with this feature.

The nest is a large, untidy structure of twigs and grass usually located in low trees or bushes. The range, as the name implies, is northern America. There is a second American species, the Loggerhead shrike, which occupies the Southeastern states. It is very similar to our Northern shrike and easily confused with it. While the range overlaps and the Loggerhead shrike is more migratory, I doubt that this bird invades the North Country to any extent.

Several people have told me that during the winter months they have had occasional visits from a shrike at their birdfeeders. Since the shrike is not a seed eater, it is probable that it is attracted by the large numbers of small birds in the area, as well as rodents that often forage around our bird feeding stations.

Before we condemn this animal let's acknowledge that predation, no matter how distasteful it may be, is a vital part of the scheme of nature. Each predator has its own place just as does each seed eater.

CHAPTER 12

All Species Valuable

Each species has its place in the scheme of things. The longer I live the more firmly I am convinced of the validity of this rule. Some organisms may appear to be more important than others but each I believe is vital.

There is a second rule or perhaps a corollary that I am beginning to feel is valid: The more lowly an organism is (in terms of our limited wisdom) the more important it is likely to be. For example, bacteria form a very lowly group in our sight. But without bacteria life as we know it on the planet could not exist.

Each time we lose a species, each time an organism becomes extinct, we suffer an irreplaceable loss. The substance of life that made that species distinct and unusual is gone, gone forever. It can never be replaced.

During the past few years there has been considerable controversy over the loss of some obscure life forms. The possible extinction of the snail darter has caused the delay in the construction of the Tellico dam in the South, while the capture and relocation of this tiny fish was accomplished. Millions of dollars were lost because of concern over this insignificant animal.

The obliteration of the habitat of the lousewort, another rare and obscure life form, also has caused the delay of a project in Maine. Again, it terms of money, the loss was great. Environmental impact surveys and statements now have to be made and accepted before certain construction projects can be undertaken. Great and unnecessary losses you say. In terms of money this may be true.

Consequences

But we have to look at these things from other than just money losses. We have to look at the possible long term consequences. What effect will the loss of the snail darter have? What great disastrous importance can the extinction of this small fish produce? Probably not much, but who can say? What good will come from our expenditures of time and money to save the lousewort? Again, who can say? Man's wisdom is tragically limited. While we have acquired vast stores of knowledge, there is yet much more to know. We have not yet learned to use this accumulation of knowledge wisely.

We cannot predict the effect of the loss of a given species. We cannot know of the benefits that I believe are most certainly there because of its existence. Carl Sagan, in a "Cosmos" episode, said something to the effect that when we cut a single thread of the ecological fabric, we have no way of knowing what thread or how many other threads will unravel.

Every day several species of plants, animals or protists disappear forever. The process is accelerating. Every day we lose genetic material that can never be replaced or duplicated. The total life gene pool becomes poorer with each passing day. It is the sum of these losses that is disastrous. It is this accumulating daily loss of many tiny bits of the stuff of life that may spell our doom.

Recent successes in gene splicing shout the necessity for preserving all genetic material. Future work with plants and animals aimed toward producing more desirable characteristics, (from the human point of view) may be severely hampered by the loss of genetic material. Disease resistance that current crop species lack may exist in their wild relatives. But if these relatives are pushed to extinction, the resistance is lost and so may be the crop species.

But I take heart. The snail darter and the lousewort stories, part of the hundreds of similar conflicts that are going on throughout our country and indeed throughout the world, give credence to the idea that maybe we are learning. Maybe we are acquiring some collective wisdom.

When you hear or read of some controversy concerning the loss of some puny, unimportant species, take the long view. Remember the corollary: the more insignificant it appears to be, the more likely it is to have significance. Remember: one extinction by itself may not be much, but the daily losses year after year may spell disaster. Take the long view. Throw your weight behind what I like to believe is our developing collective wisdom. Give it some thoughtful concern. Support all efforts to preserve all species from extinction.

CHAPTER 13

Mullein
Medical and Military

The great or common Mullein is an alien escapee. It was probably brought to the New World very early in the colonization period. It was probably brought deliberately because of its then-known medical properties. It escaped the colonial herb gardens and now inhabits almost every section of the country.

If you ever go outdoors beyond the pavement you have seen the Great Mullein. Its tall shaft, sometimes eight feet tall, is an unmistakable identification sign. The Great Mullein is a biennial, that is it takes two growing seasons to produce seeds. During the first year it is a low rosette of large leaves. These leaves may be over a foot and a half in length and up to six inches in width. This huge rosette alone should make its identification easy. If you are dealing with a smaller first year plant, a thick soft, velvety covering of fine hairs on the leaves, imparting a silvery effect will betray its identity.

The second year it puts up an unbranched stalk which has alternate leaves, large at the base decreasing in size toward the top. Stalkless, five-petaled, yellow flowers crowd together to form a spike-like arrangement about a foot long.

The Great Mullein has a world wide distribution. In the past it was widely used in the treatment of many ailments. It does have verified properties of soothing mucus membranes. An extract of Mullein is effective in relieving cough symptoms. I had an uncle once who used it as an astringent in place of styptic. While cattle will not eat it, before the days of the modern veterinarian with his tidy, compartmentalized van, Mullein extract was used to treat coughs in cattle. The leaves, fresh or dried, are the source of its cough reducing properties. The American Indian is reputed to have early recognized the demulcent and expectorant properties of this new weed. Because of its world wide distribution, it is reputed to have been used for many, many cures, from eliminating warts to protection from evil spirits, as well as all kinds of human aches, diseases and afflictions.

At about the age of ten I first became familiar with King Arthur and the Round Table. I found that the flower stalk of the Great Mullein made an admirable spear or lance. I carefully harvested a large number of these shafts, some of which were nearly six feet tall. I stored them to cure in a safe place under the eaves behind a shed. With the dried shaft as a weapon I stalked dragons in the weed patch next door. Many times I chased the Black knight, Sir Modred, over the bank and into the river armed only with my trusty Mullein lance. My lances were fairly light and stiff when dried and easy to throw. I kept invading hordes at bay by launching spear after spear into their ranks. The lightness of my lances had an additional advantage in that when one went astray and crashed into the dining room window, I never heard the sound of breaking glass.

That summer was a glorious summer as I roamed the weed and brush patches armed with a fine supply of the Great Mullein weapon.

The next year, the garden behind the shed produced a huge concentration of Mullein plants in the first year of their cycle.

Now considered mostly a pest, it once was a valued herb. Its stately stalk graces and beautifies many a weed patch. While I do not allow it to grow in my garden, I do permit it to live in out of the way nooks. Sentiment advises that I keep it around should a future Knight of the Round Table need equipment.

CHAPTER 14

Eat or Be Eaten

Eat and be eaten. Prey and be preyed upon. Throughout nature this is a constantly recurring theme. It is one of the facts of that wonderful condition we call life. Plants grow. Some are parasitized by other plants, bacteria, fungi and viruses. Some plants like the mistletoe live directly on the branches of trees. Plants are eaten by many kinds of animals. Insects consume vast amounts of plant material. Mammals, small and large, fish, birds, reptiles feed on plants.

These animals in turn provide meals for other insects, various bird, reptilian, fish and mammalian predators. Predators have their predators and they in turn theirs, until the top of the pyramid is reached. A few carnivores occupy the top niche. The top carnivors have few enemies, few species to fear.

But of course when they die, bacteria and other agents of decomposition feed on their remains. Cruel though it may seem this cycling is one of the facts that we must face and accept. We may feel angered when the owl takes the cute little cottontail that played throughout the summer around the shrubbery. We may rage at the hawk that takes the newly fledged robin. The thought of the gentle doe falling prey to a wolf or cougar may incite our wrath. But we should recognize that these are nautral occurrences that have been repeated during the eons.

Some time ago I was cutting some brush on the border of my garden. I stopped to rest and watched a white cabbage butterfly flutter by. The flight of butterflies always amazes me. It does not seem that they should be able to maneuver with such alacrity. It was about at eye level a few feet away when it was attacked by a large blue-bodied dragonfly. Dragonflies are great predators on mosquitoes and other small flying insects. But I was surprised when it attacked the white fluttering near my head.

I could hear the clash as the dry, reedy wings of the dragonfly smashed into the white vanes of the cabbage butterfly.

Perhaps because the butterfly wings were so large the dragonfly was unable to make the catch. It tried several times. When first attacked, the cabbage butterfly rose in the air. But as the attacks continued, it dropped into the nearby tall grass and weeds. Once within their protective stalks it was safe. The dragonfly tried to penetrate the tangle but each time the stalks interferred with its flying. The butterfly had found safety in a tangle that normally it would avoid.

An Escape

While I would not have minded had the cabbage butterfly been caught, since its progeny doubtless were feasting on my cabbages, I nevertheless marveled at the strategy. Here was one instance when the prey escaped, at least temporarily.

While standing quietly in my woods listening for bird calls some time ago, I heard thumping through the dry leaves. I turned my head quickly but missed the source. It nearly circled me and came to a stop in a cleared smooth patch directly to my front. It was a small frog, greyish with dark eye patches, the Wood Frog (Rana sylvatica sylvatica). This frog is a great leaper. It moves with a series of long leaps, some perhaps a yard or so in length. As I had been motionless for some time, I wondered what caused it to make such a maneuver.

Suddenly I caught a movement out of the corner of my eye. It was a rather large garter snake that was roughly following the path my frog had taken through the leaves. Apparently the stalked frog had become aware of its enemy and rescued itself with the spectacular bounding run. I watched as the snake flicked its tongue to get the frog scent.

Moving its head back and forth it appeared to pick up patches of scent here and there. But the long leaps of its intended prey left stretches devoid of any scent. I had never thought that frogs had much of a scent, but it was apparent that it had left some clues behind. Not making much progress the snake turned, circled much as my hound does when he loses a trail, to try to pick it up again at its origin. As it disappeared, the frog, which had positioned itself in an open area of good visibility left in the opposite direction. With a series of great leaps it disappeared under the low growth of the Canada May lilies that carpeted the area.

Again the predator had failed. The frog had won at least a temporary respite. I was glad that this acrobat had escaped. At the same time I was sorry to see my snake without his meal. I encourage and enjoy having snakes around my home. They are great predators of the grasshoppers that feed on my vegetables. They help keep down the population of field mice that dine on my cantaloupes. I do not begrudge the occasional bird, frog or toad that they take.

Breakfast

While walking through the woods one morning, after a rain the night before, I noticed a rather large white patch on the dark of a white pine. Investigation showed that it was a cream colored moth. Usually the brighter colored moths find hideaways during the day, but this moth was unhidden and stood out like a sore thumb. Closer examination revealed that the moth was in the clutches of a Daddy Longlegs. The Daddy Longlegs, or Harvestman, an Arachnid and not an insect, had apparently captured the moth during the hours of darkness and was just completing his breakfast.

A month or so after the frog escaped the Garter snake, I watched as a Kestrel, a sparrow hawk, flew into a pine carrying a garter snake. I hoped that it wasn't one of my snakes, but did not begrudge the diminutive sparrow hawk his meal.

And so it goes, just about everything eats and is in turn eaten. It may seem cruel but it is one of nature's facts of life. I mourn the loss of the snake that keeps the meadow mouse population down. But at the same time I am gladdened that my sparrow hawk family will be well fed. The ruffed grouse that drum and cluck in my woods occasionally make a meal for an owl or hawk, or a fox. When I chance upon a bundle of grouse feathers along side the path I am both mournful as well as happy.

The aphid feeds on my tomatoes, the ladybird beetle feeds on the aphid. A chickadee consumes the ladybird beetle. A shrike catches the chickadee. An owl dines on the shrike. This is a food chain, a slender strand of what we call the food web. These tenuous branching strands are intricately woven into a web of immeasurable complexity. Eat and be eaten is one of the very important facts of life. We cannot change it. We should not try.

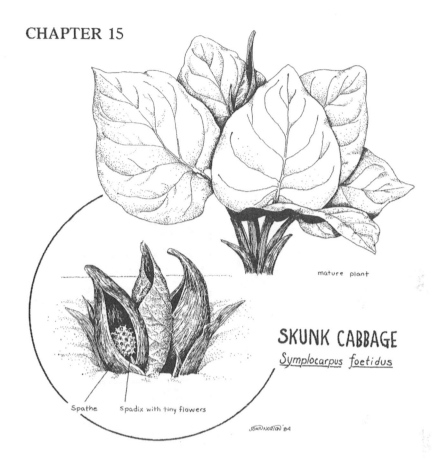

mature plant

SKUNK CABBAGE
Symplocarpus foetidus

Spathe   Spadix with tiny flowers

JOHN NORTON '84

Skunk Cabbage
Early Bloomer Smells

Except for perhaps the pussywillow, the skunk cabbage, Symplocarpus foetidus, is the earliest spring blossom you are likely to see. It is found along moist bottom lands throughout Southeastern Canada, Northeastern United States and South along the Appalachians.

In March the skunk cabbage will push its way up through the lingering snows. It has a mottled brown to purple hood which covers the blossom nestled inside. It is not much to look at but it is one of the first, and so is welcome.

35

The early blooming of this plant is not its only unique feature. There are not many brown flowers in nature so this aspect puts it in a class by itself. The name certainly is unusual. Skunk implies an odious scent. The species name foetidus, says offensive smell. And surely it does smell strong. Crush a leaf and you will release an unpleasant odoriferous vapor. The plant is aptly named.

But to me the most unusual aspect of this hardy, early bloomer is the lengths to which it has gone to insure its reproduction. Pollination is accomplished by insects. In March insects are not all that abundant. But the strong, fetid smell of rotting flesh attracts the various carrion insects. They crawl in under the purple-brown hood and accomplish the necessary pollination.

Since March is very apt to be cold with temperatures below freezing, insect activity, which is dependent on temperature, is apt to be reduced. "Foetidus" has this all worked out. It somehow maintains, within the blossom under the hood, temperatures that are above the cold surrounding environment. Ensconced in a warm, cozy boudoir, safe from the elements, the pollinating agents perform their duties and reproduction is assured.

In my early years I thought I knew the skunk cabbage. I would look at an early-growing green plant on the river bank and tell myself it was skunk cabbage. It was some years before I discovered that I was mis-labeling the False helebore (Veratrum viride). This is a poisonous plant and should never be eaten.

S. foetidus, on the other hand, is edible. The new spring leaves which appear after the blossoming, look something like small cabbage leaves, hence the name cabbage. I have been told that these leaves, if boiled in several changes of water, are quite palatable.

I have never been tempted to use this plant for food. Its odorous characteristic dampens my ardor. Nevertheless, it would seem that my ancestors might have found it a welcome change from the tedious winter diet of years ago. Skunk cabbage may have helped satisfy a late winter craving for fresh food.

Despite its rank odor, the skunk cabbage rates high on my list. I welcome its early appearance. I marvel at its reproductive devices. It is another of the many miracles of life which abound in nature. It is an astonishing example of the myriad ways in which nature copes.

CHAPTER 16

The Perfect Gift

I had been planning for many months it seemed. Actually it was probably no more than five or six weeks but at the age of six, time has a much longer span. It was the first part of February. My mother's birthday was in early March. I wanted to get her a nice gift and so some crucial plans had to be made and executed.

Herrick's general store in Glenfield had a magnificent glass case near the front of the store. It was huge. The top was above my head. There were four shelves on which were displayed one of the most glittering, shiny, fascinating collections of jewelry I have ever experienced. This treasure was flanked on one side by a candy case and on the other by a miscellaneous collection of toys, kitchen tools, etc.

I was given an allowance of five cents per week. This I was allowed to spend in what ever way I wished. I had cached a dime and two nickels and expected to have thirty to thirty-five cents by the time the birth date came around.

Each Saturday morning I got myself dressed: overshoes with pants well tucked in and tightly buckled, a heavy jacket, heavy mittens with a string through the sleeves so they wouldn't be misplaced, a staunch toque on my head and a scarf well wrapped around my neck. Unless thus attired I would never be allowed out the front door.

I then marched uptown through the vast deep troughs that had been constructed by shoveling out the sidewalks. Herrick's was not far but attired as I was, it was far enough. Once inside I would unwind the scarf and head for the jewelry display. After the first day Mr. Herrick sensed that I had a deep problem which only my pondering would solve. So he allowed me to stand undisturbed in front of the large glass pane to contemplate.

Beautiful Rings

There was a display of rings. They were very beautiful but

were well beyond my projected budget. Besides, they were small and did not show up very well. So there was no problem with that section. It was eliminated almost immediately. Mr. Herrick had a nice assortment of ladies' bracelets. While some of these were within my fiscal means, they were thin, spindly and also did not seem to show up too well.

In the center of the third shelf, just at my eye level, was a fascinating display of necklaces. There were beads of all descriptions, pearly, clear glass, colored ceramics, oval, round, cut shapes, smooth shapes, constant in size or graded. It was dazzling. The price range was vast. There were some strings below my limits and a great many above. Some were even in the one to two dollar range. After many thoughtful sessions I had narrowed the field down to a necklace of clear glass beads and one of burnt orange.

My gaze would frequently shift to the candy case or over to the miscellaneous collection on the other side, but only momentarily. My resolve was strong. I would not waver.

Inspect Necklaces

My mother's birthday came on a Saturday. On the appointed day, properly attired, although it had thawed some, I arrived at the store. Clutched in my hand inside the mitten was my entire financial resource. I went straight to the jewelry case. Mr. Herrick seemed to sense that this was the day of decision and came right over. I asked if I could inspect the two necklaces. He obliged and brought them over to a lower counter where I could see them in all their glory.

It was a hard decision. I pondered. I considered. I went back to inspect the other merchandise. The problem was finally resolved. My damp coins were on the counter. The purchase was in a small brown paper bag. My mittens and scarf were back in place and I was on my way home.

It seemed fitting that such a beautiful gift should be properly wrapped. So I immediately went to where the Christmas wrappings were stored. I selected some tissue, wrapped the gift and sealed it with some left over Christmas seals.

When she came to sit down for dinner, there beside her plate was a well wrapped package. My mother inquired if it was from me, (Who else?) and proceeded to carefully unwrap the several layers of tissue. If not too torn the tissue would go back in the box to be used again another day.

At last it was unwrapped and I watched the pleasure in her eyes and the smile on her face as she held up for all to see, a mesh bag of the shiniest, most perfect blue glass marbles, the finest gift I could buy.

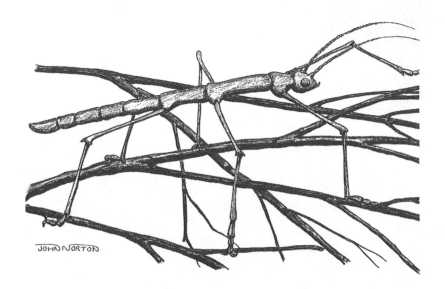

CHAPTER 17

JOHN NORTON

Walking Stick
The Stick That Walks

One time when I was in high school, I was bullhead fishing on the Black River. It was about dusk and I was comfortably ensconced on the bank with a kerosene lantern and a good supply of "Lollycapop." Lollycapop was a thick tallowy paste that served as an insect repellent. It contained citronella, some kind of tar and a host of other ingredients. It was a lacklustre unappetizing brown. Its odor was strong, strong enough to convince the wearer that it had repellent qualities but probably affecting the mosquitoes little or not at all. Where it had its effect was in the thickness with which it was applied. If thick enough the mosquito could not penetrate. So by carefully applying an even thick coat with periodic replenishing, one could get reasonable protection.

I had on my layer of protection and was intently watching my lines in the water when I saw a twig on a bush crawl along itself. Close examination showed that it was a twig with legs and a pair of antennas. I had been introduced to the walking stick.

Our local variety is about four inches long and is wingless. Two pairs of legs are spaced about an inch apart in the midsection with a third pair located at the head. Three pairs of legs identifies it as an insect. A pair of antenna sprout from the head which also features a pair of large eyes. Along the body are various bumps and projections just as any self respecting twig would have.

The camouflage is superb. When motionless, it is hard to tell the animal from the bush.

There are large numbers of walking stick species worldwide, mainly in the tropics with a few in the temperate zones. They range from a tiny toothpick sized representative to a huge tropic variety over a foot long. They are mainly herbivorous plant eaters. Our Northern New York variety is probably Diapheromera femorata. It is not abundant, probably because it tends to reproduce slowly, the female scattering from one to two hundred eggs on the ground.

While it is not abundant, it also is not rare. We rarely see it because it blends so well with its background. The next time you are looking at a bush, watch carefully. Part of it may walk away from you.

CHAPTER 18

Rhubarb
Easy Keeper, Fine Producer

I first knew it as Pie plant. I guess I was nearly twelve when the term rhubarb appeared in my vocabulary. Whatever the name, it is a valuable plant for the home gardener. It is a very long lasting perennial that will give bountiful harvests year after year. It is relatively disease and pest resistant. Properly planted, it requires a minimum of care.

There is evidence that it originated in Siberia and came to America, via Europe, in the late seventeen hundreds. There are several species. Rheum rhaponticum seems to be the species that inhabits most of our gardens.

Since it is so long lived, it is necessary that it be planted in an out-of-the-way place where it can grow undisturbed for years. It will grow in almost any soil. Once it is planted it should not be disturbed.

Thus it is wise to prepare your rhubarb bed well.

Dig a trench at least two feet deep and fill with rotted manure and compost to a depth of one foot. Pack this down well. The roots should have two or three buds at the crown. In most cases you can get good planting stock from a neighbor although there are a number of cultivars being offered by nurseries that may appeal to you. Whatever your source, plant the roots three to four feet apart, decisively firming up the rich soil. A good idea is to leave a slight dishing so that water will be directed toward the planted roots.

The hardest part comes next, waiting at least a year before you begin to harvest. Assuming you planted your row in the spring, you should be able to take a few stalks the following spring. But be patient and gentle. A second year of growth will establish your plants for severe harvesting.

The stalks should be twisted off the plant at its base. Cutting with a knife leaves a stub that may decay and infect the plant. Since the leaves are dangerous to eat, discard them immediately. They contain large amounts of oxalic acid and should go right on the compost pile. Be sure to cut off all seed stalks. These only take strength from the root. You want strong healthy roots at the end of the summer so that a plenteous supply of stalks will appear the following spring.

Now if you have done your homework and your garden work well, if you have been patient and the spirits of gardening are on your side, you can begin the third year to harvest with abandon. You will begin a pleasant relationship that will stand for many years.

Rhubarb is also known as the wine plant. If the stalks are red it makes a delicate, mild, pink wine. Or it can be combined with almost any fruit to give an infinite variety of fruity wines. A good friend was showing me her rhubarb bed which proved to be an enormous tract. I was curious as to why she had so much. She confided that she and her husband used it to make rhubarb wine and offered me a glass. It proved to be tasty. "Do you age this?" I inquired. "When we can," was her reply.

As pie material rhubarb is unexcelled. Again it can be used plain or combined with almost any fruit. My favorite is a rhubarb custard. Make your usual crust and line a nine-inch pie pan. Beat three eggs slightly and add three tablespoons of milk. Mix two cups of sugar with four tablespoons of flour and three quarters teaspoon nutmeg and add to the egg-milk mixture. Mix in 1 quart (four cups) cut up rhubarb. Pour into your pastry lined pie pan. Dot with about one tablespoon butter. Cover with pastry. Bake fifty to sixty minutes at 400°F.

For rhubarb sauce cut rhubarb in uniform pieces (¾-1"). Use one cup of water for each quart of rhubarb. Cook about ten minutes. Add one cup of sugar for each four cups of cut up rhubarb. For a delicious strawberry-rhubarb sauce add sweetened, frozen or fresh strawberries to the hot sauce. When either of these sauces are well cooked so the pulp is very soft and diluted, they make a fine refreshing drink. Rhubarb freezes well. A few packages of red cubes in the freezer will brighten the long months of winter.

Rhubarb as a slang term means a violent argument, a heated dispute. As such it is well ensconced in our sport language. But for me it means a delicious food that comes early in the year when I am champing at the bit for fresh produce. In the past nearly every home had its rhubarb bed. Because it is such an "easy keeper", because it is such an abundant producer, it still deserves a place in our gardens. I urge you to get something started if you have not already done so.

CHAPTER 19

Crow
The Uncommon, Common Crow

One of the best known birds in America is the common crow (Corvus brachyrhynchos). Not too many years back its reputation was not of the highest. It was probably least favored by farmers. There now seems to be a change in opinion.

It seems to me that the crow is no longer the villain it once was. Until recently, crows could be hunted all year long. Now it is protected except for a short, late winter season. People do not seem to see the crow as the bandit scoundrel, rascal robber, rowdy miscreant they once did.

There are several possible reasons for this change. The usefulness of the crow in insect control is much better appreciated. The reputation of the crow as an intelligent, clever animal seems to be overshadowing its villainous repute. I believe we are becoming more aware of the importance of all living things. We are beginning to understand that there is an interdependence among living things which we disrupt to our peril.

The Common or American Crow, a coal black bird, is about twenty inches long with a wing spread in excess of three feet. It usually nests high in trees, favoring conifers. The nest itself is a sturdy affair of coarse twigs and sticks. Well concealed, it is thickly lined with grasses, soft inner tree bark, and hair. Four to eight pale greenish eggs comprise the clutch. The parents are very wary and cautious when approaching the nest so as not to betray its location. I have crows nesting in my woods every year but am rarely able to find a nest.

Sign of Spring

When I was young the appearance of the first crow in early March was a sign of spring's resolute determined force. Now there are numerous crows that remain all winter. I wonder if this may not be due to the more widespread practice of spreading

44

farm manure all winter long. A swath of manure spread daily over any new fallen snow provides these birds with a fine cafeteria.

Crows are smart. I believe this aspect is what fascinates most crow fanciers. In the past the crow was relentlessly hunted. He survived because of his wariness. He became very cautious of the two-legged beast that stalked him. To get within range was a test of the skillful hunter.

A trick to stalk a sentry crow involved at least three hunters. When a sentry was spotted, the three hunters would pass behind a tree or some brush, out of sight of the sentry. Leaving one hunter behind, two would emerge and slowly circle the sentry. The sentry would also turn, watching the intruders, allowing the hidden hunter an opportunity to work himself within range. This trick, when it worked, always involved at least three hunters When tried with only two, the crow immediately became alert. His nervousness increased as the distance between the two hunters increased, eventually leading to an alarm. This can be interpreted that crows can count, at least up to two. Perhaps their counting lessons go: one, more than one.

Despite his reputation for robbing other birds' nests and pulling up planted seed corn, the crow more than pulls his weight as an insectivore. But he is a true omnivor, eating almost anything that is edible. I have read that during an abundance of insects crows gorge themselves to such an extent that flying becomes difficult. The term carrion crow attests to its habit of feeding on animals that have been killed along our highways.

Pet

The best and worst part of knowing a crow is having one for a pet. It is an experience that one will never forget. A number of years ago while walking in my woods, my hound came trotting up to me and dropped a black, wet, bedraggled ball of feathers at my feet. It was a fledgling crow, about as miserable an excuse for a bird as one could imagine.

I took him home and put him in a cloth lined box under a small light bulb for warmth. After a while he gathered his feet under himself, partially standing. This was an encouraging sign. I proceeded to try to entice him with some bread soaked in milk which he sampled after a while. Hunger eventually overcame the trauma and fright of having been in a dog's mouth and then in the totally unfamiliar surroundings of a man nest.

45

An hour or so later it was greedily taking more bread and milk. It was now standing well and inspecting its surroundings, crouching only when we came to feed it. A mashed up hardboiled egg worked into the soaked bread and later into pellets was quickly accepted. Within a day or two we were on guarded terms.

The crow, Worc, as we ingeniously began to call him, grew rapidly. The many feedings required during the day became a tiresome chore. We could miss not a single one as his raucous little voice announced each hunger pang. I looked for an alternative. When we took him for a walk, he would pick up anything that moved. He was learning to feed himself but had to be guarded from a cat and the dogs. This took up as much if not more time.

So I hit on small dog food pellets. At first he was not interested. But gradually he began to accept them and within a day or two my feeding chores were solved. A can of the pellets hidden in a planter took care of each day's feeding chores. Worc grew rapidly into a sly, clever, mischievous, rascal.

Bathing Techniques and Profanity

To know a crow one should have him as a pet. Worc was an intensely curious bird. He investigated everything. There was no nook or cranny that he did not probe. If something had the slightest glitter, it immediately acquired an investigatory priority. If it was a new shape or color, the business at hand was dropped in favor of a probe.

One day I was watering the garden. When I turned the pressure on, a thin arc of glistening water shot out over the lawn from a pinhole leak in the hose. Worc immediately spied the thin line of water glistening in the sun and flew from his vantage roof top perch to investigate.

He pecked at the drops and immediately dove in for a shower. With wings spread, he strutted in and out of the stream, splashing water across his body. Out of the shower he vigorously shook his feathers and plunged back in. This ritual went on for nearly ten minutes. At last satisfied with his hygienic performance, he flew back to his perch to preen and dry. From that time on whenever I rolled out the hose he was there at the end where the leak was to perform his ablutions.

All this was interesting and amusing, but I did not care for the leak, which progressively grew larger and was wasteful of water. At the same time I did not want to cancel the bathing ritual. Worc solved my problem within a week or two. One night I left a metal bushel basket out in the garden. Showers during the night left an inch or so of water in its bottom. Worc found this the next morning (nothing escaped his scrutiny).

Private Bath Tub

He flew to the edge of the basket and perched on the rim. After some careful consideration and a number of false movements, he dropped down into the pool. Water flew in all directions as he partook this time of a full-fledged, real bath. I walked over to see exactly what was happening.

Apparently modesty prevented him from enjoying the bath to its fullest extent as he hopped up on the rim, scolded me slightly and flew to the preening perch. Thereafter he partook of a daily bath on sunny days around noon. As the water evaporated I formed the practice of adding a quart or two and would occassionally scrub the tub out for him. He watched these operations closely from a vantage point, apparently content to let me do his housekeeping.

One evening I added several quarts bringing the level up slightly higher than normal. During the night some hard showers added to the contents until the tub was nearly half filled. At bath time the next day Worc swooped down, balanced himself on the rim and after a cursory glance at his bath water, plunged in. I happened to be near enough to clearly see what happened. His graceful dive took him to the bottom, almost out of sight. With an enormous splash, he leaped back out of the water and balanced on the rim. Water cascaded off his body as he eyed the treacherous pool.

There then ensued one of the most vile, viscious harangues I have ever heard. If there is such a thing as crow profanity, I heard the entire vocabulary. Were I able to understand the language I would probably still be blushing. Still spewing his venom, he flew back to the roof peak. There he flapped, shook and preened until his dignity had been restored. I never mentioned the incident to him as he was a very proud bird whose pride was easily damaged. But I noticed that thereafter he always carefully inspected the water level in his tub and would not enter if the level was more than an inch or two in depth.

Worc and Woodwalks

We take frequent walks through our woods. These may be for a few minutes or may last for several hours. Early in his life Worc found these excursions entertaining and interesting but somewhat difficult.

Before he learned to fly we carried him with us. After he learned to fly he would accompany us on his own. But this was difficult. Our usual pace was too fast for his waddling walk. He would shortly fall behind. When his vocal protestations would prove futile, he would launch himself into the air, fly past us and settle onto the path some yards ahead. As we caught up and passed him he would again admonish us to slow down. This usually was not effective, so he would fly ahead again. Worc enjoyed these excursions and we paid little attention to his grumblings.

Most birds do not have much in the way of food reserves during the summer months. They wake up in the morning ravenous. Worc was no exception. He was hungry and ready to go the first thing. We were an early rising family and so Worc's morning feeding was usually no problem. Someone would go out the first thing with a handful of dog food pellets to start his day. From then on he was able to alleviate his hunger pangs with insects from the garden and of course other food we offered in his food dish. Dog pellets he did not particularly relish, but when the hunger pangs were severe he would eat his fill.

Sometimes his early morning needs were filled by my young offspring. They got into the habit of letting the crow into their bedroom through a window. We had a rule about having the crow in the house, making this a somewhat illegal maneuver.

Expensive Taste

Knowing that there were people inside doing nothing, Worc very early learned to get them up by tapping on the screen or window pane. Awakened, an offspring would quietly take a pellet of hamburger from the refrigerator. Then in the security of their room they would open the window to the waiting crow, who would then hop inside and dine sumptuously. Once, when the hamburger, which had been purchased especially for the crow, had been depleted, he was fed ground chuck by an errant offspring. Thereafter he disdained plain hamburger. I put a stop to this expensive taste and Worc, with great reluctance and even greater protestations, went back to dog pellets.

One morning the whole family was late in getting up. The limits of Worc's patience had been reached. He was hungry and wanted to be fed. Apparently his entreaties at the bedroom window produced no results. I was awakened by his raucous cawing in the living room. I jumped up with a start. The crow in the living room would result in considerable havoc at best, untold disaster at the worst.

I rushed into the living room which was filled with his demanding caws but no crow was visible. Suddenly I knew the answer. He was perched on the chimney outside, communicating down the fireplace flue. Many times he had heard our voices coming up the flue. Apparently it seemed logical that he could reach us in the same manner. "I'll be right out, Worc," I shouted up the chimney. I grabbed a handful of dog pellets and as I stepped out the garage door Worc swooped down from the chimney to light on my arm and gobble up his breakfast cereal. And so, with bated breath we started another day with our mischievous, unpredictable black beauty.

Truces Are Struck

In addition to being curious, Worc had a teasing streak, a pestering, harassing mode that gave us amusement, discomfort and once almost did him in. When he was young, we had to protect him from our cat.

But as he grew his size seemed to intimidate our feline. One day when the cat thought she had him cornered, he flew directly at her, pecked her severely on the head and continued to drub her with his wings as she scampered under a lawn chair for protection. After that incident, Worc had no problems with the cat.

49

Whenever he flew over, she skulked for cover. Whenever he strutted around the lawn, she left the environs.

He seemed to regard the lawn as a playground and an arena in which to perform his harassments. During the afternoons on sunny days, my family was wont to sunbathe. One or more in bathing suits or other scanty garb would lie on lawn chairs soaking up the ultraviolet. Worc was intrigued and circled the bathers. Each circle became tighter. His head would cock as something caught his eye needing close inspection. With dignity and decorum he approached, ever closer, at last walking under the outstretched and unsuspecting sunbather.

Our lawn chairs are of the wide webbed variety with large unsupported squares through which projected glistening chunks of naked flesh. These lovely, intriguing protrusions were too much to be denied. Worc attempted to salvage some for his own use. The sunbather in question, rudely aroused from a pleasant drowsy siesta, would leap from the chair with howls of anguish. Worc, the first time, hastily ran from under the chair, then flew to the chimney.

Stalking Fun

There he surveyed the scene below, the clenched fists of the injured party and the laughter of those nonparticipants. When things settled down he flew back to the lawn and proceeded to again stalk a sunbather. This became great fun over the rest of the summer. The sunbathers almost as wily as the crow, learned to drape a blanket over the chair such that the glistening, tempting flesh squares were hidden and access to the underneath was denied. Even then Worc would sometimes sneak up and sample a portion of glistening thigh, immediately flying to his chimney perch to caw his derision at the irate bather below.

At the time I had a gentle hound, the best rabbit dog I ever owned. He would hunt all day until so tired that he could hardly crawl up on the seat of the Jeep to go home. If I could make him hear me, he would come even if on a hot track, which eliminated long cold waits at the end of the day. Tobe was in his declining years the summer Worc stayed with us. He liked to use the lawn to sunbathe as did my family. He would spend hours completely relaxed on the soft grass enjoying the leisure he had earned the winter before.

Worc was respectful of Tobe, probably since Tobe was several times larger than he. But the inert furred form with its occassionally twitching tail piqued his curiosity. A number of times he inspected Tobe from a distance, gradually edging closer. The occasional twitch of the tail was overpowering and at last he gave it a tweak, immediately hopping into the air and flying to the picnic table.

Tobe's reaction was sluggish and indifferent which emboldened Worc. He returned for a second try and then a third. At the last try, Tobe jumped to his feet as Worc flew to his chimney. This time Worc was silent. There were no derisive taunting caws. Tobe moved to another place on the lawn and went back to sleep. From then on Worc gave Tobe a considerable portion of his attention. At first he was careful not to go too far, but as Tobe was a gentle dog and hard to arouse, Worc became more daring and bold.

Midday Havoc

This went on for several weeks. Tobe's midday siestas were in havoc, his patience had about run its course. One afternoon after a good session of weeding in the garden, I was sitting in a lawn chair enjoying a respite from the hot sun. Tobe was napping in the lush grass across the lawn. Worc was sitting in a lawn chair beside me, eying a frosty glass of iced tea. When he was convinced that I was not about to share any of it, he flew over to Tobe landing a few feet away. The overflight apparently warned Tobe, for as Worc started his usual circular stalk, Tobe was on his feet taking the astonished bird in his mouth. Tobe gave him a couple of shakes and dropped the wet, ruffled mass of feathers in the grass. Tobe walked to the other side of the lawn to continue his siesta.

The crumpled sodden lump made no movement. Saddened, I thought, "Well crow, you asked for it." I was about to go over and assay the damage when I caught a slight movement. A beady eye peered above the grass. Then the head came up and slowly surveyed the lawn. It concentrated on Tobe well away on the other side. Satisfied that the enemy was at a safe distance, he slowly brought a wing back into place. The other wing, grotesquely distorted at an angle, slowly resumed its normal shape. On his feet, Worc surveyed the scene. He gave himself a cursory preening and with great dignity (as though nothing had happened) walked to the drive where he searched briefly for some nonexistent food. Having established that nothing out of the ordinary had happened, he flew back to his chimney.

51

From that day on, Worc never harassed Tobe. A truce had been struck. Worc had taught the cat a lesson. Tobe had taught Worc a lesson. Peace had been established among our animals.

Combined Avian and Canine Tactics

Worc was not allowed in the house. When he was young and could not fly he was reared indoors. But as he began to try his wings we took him outside. He left a trail of too many overturned lamps and vases. After he learned to fly, he was relegated to the outdoors where he soon occupied the garage as his abode.

But as with all good rules, they got broken from time to time. Sometimes someone would bring him inside. Sometimes he would walk in through an accidentally opened door. Our usual procedure was to let him wander for a few minutes before returning him to the outdoors. An unwritten rule evolved that whoever was responsible for letting him in had to clean up after him. He was totally unbiased as to where he left his droppings.

He seemed to do a lot of talking whenever he came inside. This cackling and rumbling was more or less constant except when a daughter was playing the piano. As she played he would sit quietly, perched on the back of a chair or sometimes on the top of the piano. He would watch her fingers as they moved over the keys listening intently to the various chords. When she stopped playing to leaf through her music he would hop down to the keyboard taking great delight whenever such a hop produced sound. He would prance up and down the keys pounding out his sonatas. It seemed that we tired of hearing his music long before he tired of playing it.

Grooming

Many animals have grooming behavior patterns where one animal will groom itself or another in some manner. Our pet crow, in addition to grooming himself, frequently groomed members of my family. When a progeny was sunbathing on a lawn lounge, Worc would drop from the roof to a delicate landing on the exposed chest. He would look everything over carefully satisfying himself that all was in order and then address himself to the face that was attached to the chest he was occupying.

52

Joint Manuevers

Very carefully he would groom the eyebrows. With little short snaps of the bill he would gently move across each eyebrow carefully laying the hairs in place and softly massaging the flesh. When the occupant closed his eyes Worc would, with great care, delicately straighten out the eye lashes. This was all done with the care, understanding and skill of a surgeon. My offspring reported that it was a pleasant experience which they enjoyed several times each week.

I have read many stories about animals cooperating with one another in some endeavor. Usually they describe activities among animals of the same species. I do not often read of cooperation between species except for the many instinctive symbiotic relationships. However, I was able to witness another interesting cooperative effort of this between my dogs and Worc. We live well off the main road in splendid isolation. Neighboring dogs occasionally wander in to check our activities. Once they invade the territory of my dogs, the fur begins to fly.

One sunny afternoon a large strange dog trotted down our drive ignoring the territorial signs that my dogs had carefully posted throughout my woods. Tobe, the hound, was laying in the grass on the lawn. Arrow, who was a very mixed breed of collie and several other strains, was asleep in his dog house. Worc spied the intruder and gave the alarm. Something in the tone of his cry immediately alerted the two dogs who were on their feet to confront the visitor.

The intruder was a very large dog, so their challenge was somewhat subdued. The dogs circled, stiff-legged, posturing, sending signals, neck and back hackles upright, waiting for the die to be cast. The match was pretty even, with one small and one medium sized dog pitted against one large animal. The large stranger, being on foreign territory, was perhaps at a slight disadvantage. The confrontation seemed to be at a stalemate when out of the blue came Worc.

From the top of a pine tree he launched himself straight at the head of the intruder. Broadcasting loud excited caws, he sounded the charge. With both his flanks exposed to our dogs and being dive-bombed in a frontal assault by heaven knows what, the aplomb and bravado of the alien canine vanished. He bolted with the two smaller dogs at his heels and the crow flying a few feet ahead cawing with all the relish and excitement that a military rout can bring.

The last I saw of them they were well down the road with the strange dog conducting a relatively successful but harried and very undignified retreat, the pursuers barking and cawing in the delicious excitement of total victory.

CHAPTER 20

JOHN NORTON

Chokecherry
Fruit for Small Boys

It is a shame that the common chokecherry (Prunus virginiana) is not a more palatable fruit. It is widespread from shore to shore and border to border. It grows well in almost any soil. Most years it bears abundantly. In short, it is almost an ideal fruit. But it is puckery. My mouth puckers up as I write these words. Yet its memory is pleasant. I fondly remember warm days of late August and chokecherries.

Chokecherry bushes in bloom in the spring are a precious sight. The clusters of blossoms on a long stem or raceme may literally cover the plant. There does not seem to be much scent involved but bees find the blossoms and busily take advantage of the harvest.

These racemes result in clusters of pea-sized fruit turning

from green to red and finally to black when fully ripened. The darker they get the less puckery the taste. The chokecherry is used as food by many birds. This is probably why it is so widespread. The hard, undigested seeds are dispersed in ever widening circles from an existing patch as birds distribute their droppings after feasting.

I discovered the chokecherry when I was about seven years old. The berries looked very inviting and I sampled some one warm July day. The result was not pleasant. A more mature and experienced friend of ten or twelve advised that I wait until the cherries were darker. "The blacker the better", was his sagacious advice.

Within a few weeks the cherries began to darken. I searched for the bushes with the blackest fruits, quickly learning the secret. On our way from the old swimming hole we always passed a long section loaded with chokecherry bushes. It was great delight to sample the fruits after the gentle and pleasant fatigue of an afternoon swim. Finding a shrub with dark fruit, we would cut a well ladened branch, find a grassy spot, lie back and watch the cumulus clouds as they made faces across the sky.

'Sweet' Fruit

Occasionally someone would discover a bush that had especially sweet fruit. This discovery was not broadcast but usually was shared with a close friend. In any event, whether the fruit was especially sweet or not, the first taste always caused a puckering. No matter how sweet or ripe the fruits are there is always an astringent quality with which one must contend. Usually after the first cluster or two the mouth becomes accustomed to the astringency and from then on one can eat with almost complete impunity.

There was one hazard as I recall. If one imbibed excessively, the teeth began to darken. This was not a permanent effect but it did serve to inform one's elders that chokecherries had been on the menu.

Some parents frowned on the eating of this fruit which of course made it all the more delectable. I do not recall that my parents had any doubts about the fruit or that I ever experienced any harmful effects. But I do remember the dismay on my mother's face as I showed up for an evening meal, with parental guests, prominently displaying a mouth full of black teeth.

Chokecherries do make a fine jelly. Using one cup of water to each quart of crushed fruit (don't crush the pits) bring to a boil, then simmer for about half an hour. Strain and use according to your usual pectin recipe. This makes a dark jelly that is quite tasty on a January morning when the temperature is below zero and warm summer days are but a memory or a hope.

Probably the most important use of the chokecherry is as food for birds and small boys. Lying back on a grassy slope, young males consume handfuls of juicy black cherries and skillfully propel the pits at a mark on the road side. The loser in the contest has to replenish the supply of food and ammunition. The winners continue to contemplate the flat bottomed cumulus ships that sail overhead. The warm days of late summer, the lack of worries and cares of the ten-year-old and a supply of ripe chokecherries combine in an unbelievable synergism.

CHAPTER 21

Snow Flea
Living Soot

A number of years ago I was in the depths of a swamp on snowshoes. My hound was out of hearing. I was savoring the perfect quiet that one finds in the winter swamp. It was a mild day in February. The snow was soft and "packy."

A fresh snowfall the night before had decorated the trees. The sun was shining. It was one of those rare days when everything seemed to come together. But something was amiss. Although there had been a fresh snow, much of the snow was covered with what looked like soot.

I thought that I was miles away from any human habitation. It did not seem possible that there was any nearby source of soot. Puzzled, I scooped up a handful of the dusky snow for a closer look. It was not soot nor any other particulate matter, but tiny living creatures. As I watched they crawled around on my handful of snow. They made prodigious leaps of many times their own length. I was looking at snow fleas (Achorutes nivicolus).

I looked more carefully at the snow at my feet. In the small hollows it was jet black. Thousands of these little forms of life

58

crowded into massive jamborees. Hundreds of thousands littered the snow all around.

Since that time I've noticed this living soot almost anywhere on the snow when there was a thaw in effect. Sometimes puddles in the early spring will be completely covered with a sheen of living black. As the temperature drops they disappear to reappear with the next thaw. They are so small that after the snow is gone they become inconspicuous. Several of these minute insect specks could easily share the head of a pin.

No Relation

While called snow fleas, this animal is no relation to the dog or cat flea. It does not bite and is harmless. You don't have to try to avoid it. It will avoid you.

The snow flea lives in the duff, on or just below the soil surface. It is so tiny that it can crawl about in the soil spaces between soil particles. When a thaw signals the correct conditions it crawls up through the snow structure finding ample passage between snow and ice crystals. As the temperature drops it retreats to warmer conditions under the snow on the forest floor.

The snow flea is a wingless insect member of the springtail family. Springtails use a special forked structure (the furcula) arising from the ventral side of the fourth abdominal segment. It is folded forward and held in place on the third segment by a sort of clasplike device (the tenaculum). The springtail launches itself by extending the furcula downward and backward. As a result of this, prodigious jumps of perhaps fifty times its own body length are achieved.

Snow fleas are found almost everywhere there is dead and decaying vegetation on the soil. They feed on molds, algae, decaying substances and are considered beneficial to the forest in the reducing of litter and subsequent formation of humus. They exist in unimaginable numbers. In some places hundreds of millions may occupy a few square yards.

The next time you see soot blackened fresh snow, take a closer look. If the soot crawls and jumps, you have been introduced to the snow flea.

CHAPTER 22

The Flexible Flyer

My first hand-sled was a small nondescript affair with the steering handle right up front over the crossbar. It was slow and hard to steer. Some of the kids had better models which were the object of considerable admiration. My heart's desire soon settled on the possession of one of these beauties.

I carefully explained the merits of this sled to my mother who agreed as to the quality but remained noncommittal about its acquisition. As Christmas approached that year, my explanations became open requests. My mother listened carefully but made no commitment. My hopes rose and fell. I soared when she seemed to agree. I plunged when offered arguments. Christmas eve came and I put on my "PJs" with no clear decision in sight.

But on Christmas morning there it sat in front of the tree, my "Flexible Flyer." The runners and the metal braces were a brilliant red. The hardwood slats glistened with varnish. The steering bar, also of sturdy hardwood, was located back from the two-piece black front crossbar. Thus positioned it was so linked as to make steering easier.

The runners were concaved, a new, important and very desirable innovation, a new word in my vocabulary. The back ends of the runners were bent in a tight curve, a new safety measure. It was a masterpiece, everything that I had desired.

Sledding was poor that day. I spent most of the afternoon lying on my belly on the sled in front of the Christmas tree, twisting the steering arms to "loosen up the steering." The sled needed a rope. My mother offered a length of used clothesline. I pointed out that such a fine sled deserved a fine rope so she let me cut a piece from a hank of brand new line.

I threaded the line through the hole at the end of the steering arms and tied a knot so it would not pull back through. Back through the other hole on the opposite end of the arm, adjusting the loop so that it would fit loosely between the slats and not drag on the ground.

A piece of fine grit emery cloth (to minimize scratches) removed the paint from the concave portions of the runners. A probably needless drop of oil from the sewing machine drawer on the steering joints completed my vehicle preparation. All of these procedures I had gleaned from listening to the bigger boys discuss the merits of sleds and the techniques of sledding. Two or three days after Christmas the weather changed and good sledding became a possibility. Bundled up, pulling my handsome sled behind me, I headed for "Phelps" hill.

Phelps hill was an ideal hill for hand sledding. Very steep for the first few feet, it gradually leveled off on to a long level stretch. With a good "slam" one could go almost to the blacksmith shop. The better sled and sledders would go well beyond out into the road.

That was a fantastic winter. I was just old enough to be allowed to go to the hill by myself. I had one of the fastest sleds in town. I was almost invincible at the game of sled tag. On weekends and after school I exhausted myself. After each session my precious sled was stored each night on the front porch away from the elements, but where I could check on it through the living room window.

Over the several years when hand sledding was at its height for me, my "Flexible Flyer" was a constant winter companion. Each spring before it was stored away for the summer I gave it a coat of varnish from the big gallon can that my mother used to touch up the floors. The red paint gradually became chipped. Our old paint collection did not contain any red paint and I could not afford to buy any so I contented myself with applying oil to the bare spots.

Somewhere along the line, I stopped using my flyer. One winter it never got out of storage. Other things filled my time. It remained in a back corner gathering dust. I don't know what became of it. Probably it was donated to some charity drive. But I still see it standing in the porch corner waiting patiently for me to come out and play.

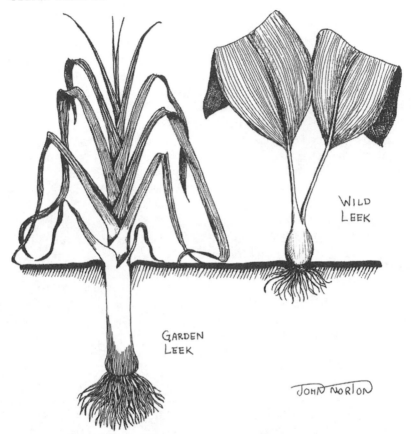

CHAPTER 23

WILD
LEEK

GARDEN
LEEK

JOHN NORTON

Leeks
Leeks "Bait" the Breath

When I was in the third grade, the expanding four-room school held two grades per room. My third grade occupied a room with the fifth graders. We enjoyed a long noon hour allowing the "Town kids" to go home for the noon meal.

For a number of students the route home during the spring months passed through some meadows and a woods. One day, during the leek season, a group of returning students feasted on these wild delicacies on their return from their noon meal. When consumed raw, this native onion is sweet and easy to eat, but it leaves a residue.

The wild leek (Allium tricoccum) has a widespread habitat. It grows abundantly from Northern New England and Southern Canada south as far as North Carolina and west to Iowa and Minnesota. In the spring it puts forth a small spear of tightly rolled leaves which remind one of the domesticated leek. This early growth is very edible and choice.

As the season progresses the leaves unroll producing flat leaves up to ten inches in length and one to three inches wide. In this condition they do not resemble the onion with its tubular leaves. By the end of June most of the evidence of a leek bed vanishes. But if you have marked its location the bulbs make for additional good eating.

As the allium-stuffed students returned to the school room, their arrival became apparent instantaneously. One leek scented student was barely tolerable, half a dozen made the room unbearable. As with all onion eaters, these students were immune to their diffusing scent. They feigned unawareness of the cause of our ruffled and twisted noses.

Saraphena Rinkenburg, tall, thin, regal, ruled the third and fifth grades with an iron hand. She was a veteran of the school room. She had shepherded generations of students through the various grades. She was gentle, understanding and tolerant but also stern, brooking no nonsense. I have many fond memories of this fabulous lady. During the third, fifth and then the sixth grades she exerted an influence that greatly shaped my life. Tolerant and understanding as she was, she could not stand the reeking stench that a half dozen mischievous fifth graders exuded as they waited with "baited" breath, as it were, her impending dictum.

The admonishment was swift and appropriate. After a stern public lecture, they were sent home with notes to their parents. I expect that she felt the parents should also suffer the penetrating fragrance. The next day, slightly chastened and still slightly perfumed, but at least tolerable, the group returned. As I recall, only one tried to repeat the trick. He spent two days in the furnace room struggling with extra homework.

The wild leek, A. Tricoccum, is not the same onion as the domesticated garden leek. The domesticated leek, A. perrum, is much more mild in flavor. It has a soft bulb which, when grown with some skill, produces a beautiful, thick stalk ten or more inches in length. This onion makes great vichyssoise or in more common language, potato-leek soup. It is quite hardy and if properly heeled and mulched in the garden during the winter months, it can be harvested for delicious early spring eating. It does not carry with it the capacity to stain one's breath.

It seems to me that fewer people take advantage of the spring wild leek harvest than when I was young. Fewer persons now enjoy the delicacy and, of course, risk its perils. I suppose this is called progress.

CHAPTER 24

JOHN NORTON

Trout Bird
The Trout Bird Is Calling

I first knew him as the "trout bird."

When I was about nine or ten a good friend took me trout fishing back in the western foothills of the Adirondacks. I was standing at the base of a waterfall and had just caught a nice trout. I sat on the bank to admire the brilliant spots and the red-orange fins of my catch. I was feeling quite satisfied when this lovely, plaintive song drifted down to us from high in a nearby balsam. We both paused, listening for the song to come again. Then it came, a haunting, almost sad refrain of about six notes.

"That's a trout bird," said my friend and so it has been for me ever since. I now know that I was listening to the white-throated sparrow. Each spring when this sleek sparrow sings his melancholy song to me, I'm transported back to that sand bar with the sound of falling water, the smell of balsam and a fine trout in my fish basket.

The white-throated sparrow is known in New England as the Peabody bird. His song is said to say "Sam Peabody-peabody-peabody". I've never been successful in matching other people's words to bird songs. I cannot match peabody to this beautiful refrain but the tune without words is fixed in my memory.

The most distinctive feature of this handsome sparrow, as the name implies, is the white on the throat. There are several bands of white and black on the high crown of the bird with patches of yellow from the bill to each eye.

The rest of the bird, as a friend once said, is sparrow colored. The only other bird with which the white-throated sparrow might be confused is the white-crowned sparrow which also, as the name implies, has black and white stripes on the head but with a greyish throat. Neither of these birds seems to have any streaks or stripes on the breast.

The white-throated sparrow usually nests on the ground but may use low bushes. Four or five brown spotted pale green eggs are commonly laid. As with most sparrows, the main diet is weed seeds. Insects do find their way into the diet but the vast bulk of their food consists of seeds. It breeds from the northern states to the Canadian tree line. Our Adirondacks support a substantial breeding population. Migration takes it to the southern states, Florida and southern Texas.

For me it is one of the many harbingers of spring. When I hear its sweet wistful song I know it is time to head for the trout stream. The trout bird is calling.

CHAPTER 25

JOHN NORTON

Hemlock
Think Music

In the early days the hemlock was very abundant. The trees were huge and numerous. Since other tree varieties were also abundant and much more desirable, the hemlock was considered a nuisance, a weed. It was used mainly by the tanning industry, as hemlock bark was found to contain large amounts of tannin.

Large amounts of bark were necessary as was a good supply of water. Thus most tanneries were located on clear running streams near supplies of hemlock bark.

One time many years ago, I was fishing on the Independence River with a friend. We took a shortcut on our return and passed through an area where there were many huge tree trunks lying on the ground. My first thought was that a great storm might have caused the disaster or that a fire might have been involved. But the stumps showed clean cuts. They had been sawn. The trees had been felled by some woodsman and left where they fell to rot.

I wondered out loud and my companion informed me that these were hemlock trees that had been felled for their bark. Since hemlock is somewhat rot resistant, many of the logs were still in fair shape. We estimated that those trunks had been on the ground for at least seventy-five years. I was appalled by the waste.

Apparently only the bark had been taken. The loggers had cut down these trees, taken only the bark, and left the huge trunks to rot. In the early days we thought that there would always be trees to cut, to exploit.

The eastern hemlock, sometimes called the Canada hemlock, is a beautiful evergreen. It is a tall tree, ranging to fifty, even eighty feet in height. The mature tree has long slender branches that gracefully droop toward the ground. If growing in the open the lowest branches often droop so as to touch the ground.

The Eastern hemlock (tsuga canadensis), a conifer, has short flat needles that are soft and blunt as compared with the spruces. Its delicate and inconspicuous flowers are produced in the spring with the small cones maturing by fall. These cones rarely exceed an inch in length and ripen to a reddish brown. The hemlock spruce, another name that it goes by, is very tolerant of a variety of light conditions.

It will grow reasonably well in full sun and does itself proud where shade is a problem. Its wood is brittle and coarse in grain. It warps and splinters easily. Its knots are very hard. It is used for pulp and to construct boxes, pallets and crates.

From this you might conclude, as did many of our forefathers, that it is not much of a tree. However, when you consider the graceful upright stance, the delicate lacy foliage, the rich dark green color and its adaptability, it has to be regarded as one of our finest trees.

One text I consulted describes the eastern hemlock as "music in the form of a tree." I think this says it all about the hemlock. First considered a weed and even now not regarded as having much commercial value, the hemlock finds its place in beauty and poetry. The canadensis deserves a much higher place in our regard. When you next see a hemlock, think music.

68

CHAPTER 26

JOHN NORTON 1984

The Palmer Method
It Never Really Worked

My handwriting is and always has been terrible, if not atrocious. Way back in my early school days teachers recognized this failing. They had to. They couldn't recognize anything that I wrote. Penmanship was something that everyone had to do. Because of my lack of skill I had to practice penmanship considerably more than did other students. I hated it but struggled as best I could.

The Palmer method was in vogue. It seems to have started around the turn of the century. Its stylized loops and curves were supposed to enable one to develop a grace and an ease with handwriting. I never developed any grace and handwriting never came easy. As I recall there were two basic moves that one practiced.

69

One was a series of "O's" that were happily traced across the page between two ruled lines. The result was similar to a coiled spring. The other exercise was a series of slanted up and down lines, again traced between two ruled lines across the page. The result here was like a tight, fine picket fence.

I labored hard and long with these two exercises. But my circles were not symmetrical and even and each one of the miserable ovals went above or below the proper line, or both. My fences were ragged, uneven, spotty and showed a lack of concentration, so one teacher told me. "Use your forearm, not your wrist," I was told again and again.

I tried using the arm but it was tiring and not easy to control. I was shown samples of how the exercises should look, samples that were done by two girls who were famous for their "springs and fences." I had to admit they were marvels of symmetry and accuracy. They looked just like the examples in the book. Then one day disillusion set in.

Because of my lack of progress I was required to spend part of the noon hour practicing. Each new lesson started with a line of springs and then a line of fence. The two model girls were also in the room with me getting ready for the afternoon's lesson. For some reason I looked over to see what they were doing to find that they were transcribing their springs and fences between two rulers held on the limiting lines. Their efforts were not free-handed at all. True, their freehand products were vastly superior to mine, but the exercises they handed in were not strictly honorable. I tried the same trick but did not hand in my efforts. I decided they looked too good, that surely I would be found out. Besides, now that I knew the Palmer stars were not infallible, I was not as concerned about my efforts.

The second disillusionment came one day as I stood by the teacher's desk while she corrected a paper I had handed in. I was astounded to see that she did not use her arm but wrote with her wrist. I was tempted to point this out, but resisted that triumph. Instead, I returned to my seat secure with my new knowledge.

I did not cease my efforts. I was not allowed to. Each new teacher, thinking she would succeed where others failed, provided me with a new, slim, red book with its flowing lines. Under each dedicated teacher I practiced my circles and my fences. I did my loops and slants and a myriad of other things for each troubled soul until discouraged, she turned to something else. Oh, my writing improved with the years. While it is not fit for public consumption, it can easily be read by those who have had special training.

The typewriter was my salvation. I never became very good at it but at least my writing was legible. With my trusty portable I was able to finish high school, graduate from college and survive the Army. I carried my battered old Royal all over the world and communicated with the high and mighty as well as the peons with a minimum of disgrace.

I have read recently that because of the demise of the Palmer method and the resulting sloppy handwriting of the average American, forgers are having difficulty practicing their art. Instead of graceful, flowing loops common to one and all, each writer has developed an individuality that is difficult to duplicate. So at last I triumph. My distinctive style has its merits. I no longer worry that some nefarious individual will duplicate my scrawl with ease. I no longer am concerned that my signature will appear on documents without my permission. Now if I could only learn to spell.

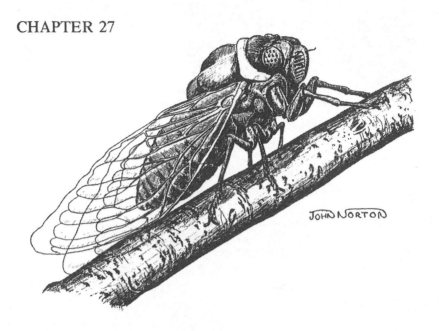

JOHN NORTON

Cicada
Rip Van Winkle of the Insect World

For me, one of summer's most nostalgic sounds is the shrill, ringing cry of the cicada. When the metallic ring breaks the heat of a summer day, I am transported back to my school days, to a drowsy summer Sunday on the front porch.

Few are awake, fewer are moving. It is a time for rest, inactivity, contemplation. I can see myself watching the dancing heat waves that curl off the macadam ribbon that went through town. I feel a sadness that those days are gone, a gladness that I experienced them.

The penetrating cry of the cicada is made by one of the most sophisticated and complex sound producing mechanisms in the animal kingdom. It is produced only by males who are known as the noisiest insects in the world. This insect, so terrifying in appearance, is harmless. It is a large insect measuring up to two inches in length.

It looks like a winged bullet flying backward. The blunt end, the forward end, features two enormous eyes. The clear, plastic like wings are large and when at rest fold well back beyond the posterior of the animal. Our variety is black and green with grey underneath.

There are two groups in the family cicadidae, so classified on the length of their life cycles. The periodical cicadas have the longest life cycles. There are two varieties with cycles of seventeen and thirteen years. The seventeen year locusts, as they are sometimes called, are not locusts at all but are related to the aphids or plant lice.

A 'Marvel'

The name locust appears to have been applied by the Pilgrims when, in addition to their other hardships, they were subjected to the emergence of a brood of these periodicals. The periodicals are distributed in scattered patches throughout the eastern United States. The thirteen year variety is largely southern.

The emergence of the larva is a marvel of synchronization. Even though the eggs were laid over a period of several weeks seventeen years earlier, the larva all emerge within a few hours. Although the length of the cycle varies by several years, the two varieties all go through five metamorphic stages. When the appointed time comes, usually late in May to mid-June, the grubs emerge from the ground and climb on the nearest vertical surface. The insect pauses. A split appears along the back and the final, the adult, form emerges. The wings unfold. After a rest period, during which the wings dry, the adult is ready for the final act in its cycle.

The emergence of a brood is something to behold. Hundreds, thousands of insects will emerge at once. The ground will be pierced from below with large holes as the grubs climb out. Trees, buildings, poles, fences will be covered with molting animals, leaving behind their empty shell. The sound gradually builds up to a continuous crescendo.

Mating takes place. The female makes slits in the twigs of trees and deposits her eggs. She may make several depositories leaving perhaps five hundred eggs. This adult stage may last a month or so. After six to eight weeks the eggs hatch and the larva drop to the ground. They bury themselves in the soil, remaining there for thirteen or seventeen years, feeding on tree roots and the cycle repeats.

73

Little Harm

They do little harm. They cannot sting or bite you. The twigs in which the eggs are laid may die. The roots on which they feed may be damaged. But there appears to be no permanent harm done to plants or animals. Since the broods of the periodicals are widely scattered, but very concentrated in small areas, they are greatly subject to man's depredations. Some well known broods have failed to appear. It appears that in some areas some broods are being excavated away or paved over.

The other major group, the Dog Day Cicadas, are the ones we are most likely to encounter in the North Country. These have a much shorter life cycle, ranging from two to five years. These cycles are staggered so that some adults appear each summer during July and August. This appearance during the later part of summer, the dog days of summer, accounts for their common name.

To some they are known as Harvest Flies or Jaw Flies. Except for the time under ground and their emergence during the later part of the summer and their reduced numbers, their life cycles are essentially the same as the Periodical cicadas.

You reach into a shrub to pick a flower. A resting cicada takes alarm and bursts forth with a rush of wings. The suddenness of the flight, the noise of the flight and the size of the insect will startle you even if you know it is there. But it will do you no harm. Its sound is a talisman adding to the magic of summer. The cicada you are seeing is a close relative of the seventeen year miracle, another of nature's marvels.

CHAPTER 28

Switchel
Kool Aid in the Eighteen Hundreds

The term "pitching hay" used to mean hard, hot work. It meant working in the hot sun during July and August forking hay on to wagons in the hay fields and later unloading the hay in hot barns. This hot, hard work demanded copious supplies of thirst quencher.

Somewhere in the past, switchel evolved as an effective, reasonably inexpensive, tasty, palatable answer. My grandmother used to tell me how she would at mid-morning and mid-afternoon take an earthen jug of switchel out to the men in the hay field. The drink was welcomed and the jug drained forthwith.

When I asked how it tasted, she made me a sample. Some vinegar, sugar and a little ginger in a cold glass of water were the ingredients as I recall. Oh, it did taste good. But then anything my grandmother made for me tasted good. I would relish foods at her table that I could hardly stand at home.

I finally grew up, physically that is, and forgot about switchel. One hot July day I came home from shearing Christmas trees. Sweaty, thirsty and in need of liquid, switchel popped into my mind. I proceeded to concoct a glass and to relish its contents. From then on, that was my hot weather thirst quencher.

As with many things, I sought to experiment and try to improve on the formula. I have kept a hive or two of bees for many years and decided to try some of my honey as the sweetener. I have finally arrived at a recipe which I feel should take a prize in the Betty Crocker cookoff.

Take about two teaspoons of honey dissolved in a few tablespoons of hot water. Add three to four tablespoons of cider vinegar. All these quantities are relative and you'll have to adjust to suit your own taste. But the cider vinegar is a must. The apple flavor of the vinegar somehow blends with the honey and gives a gentle spiciness suggestive of ginger, but not as harsh. Pour in ice cold water, stir and drink. If it hits you like it does me, you'll immediately start on a second glass.

75

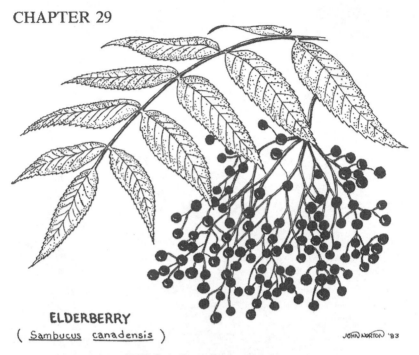

CHAPTER 29

ELDERBERRY
(Sambucus canadensis)

JOHN NORTON '83

Elderberry
A Superb Pie Filling

The elderberry can be found almost anywhere. It is a tall shrub ranging from six to ten or more feet in height. It seems to prefer a rich moist soil, but it can be found in many other locations. The sprawling stems, which grow in thick clumps, are brittle and pithy.

In June and July it is covered with tiny white blossoms that are arranged in broad flat-topped clusters. These clusters may be several inches across. Thus adorned, it is a spectacular sight. The leaves are compound. That is, several leaflets are born on a single leaf stalk. These leaves are produced opposite one another on the plant stalk.

You can start savoring the elderberry during its blossoming season by harvesting these blossom clusters for a delicious dessert. Dipped in a batter, deep fried and rolled in powdered sugar, they make a gourmet event out of a plain meal.

Probably the widest use of the elderberry is in making elderberry wine. Almost any wine recipe using fruit can be used substituting elderberries. The result will satisfy even the most sophisticated home vintner.

My favorite elderberry product is elderberry pie. This delicacy will remind one of a good blueberry pie. But is has something more. The color leans more toward a red-purple. The tiny flavorful berries give a slightly different consistency. The flavor is delicate, different from the blueberry yet similar, and there is the delicious hint of almond. I can't describe it. You'll just have to try it for yourself.

My greatest problem with elderberry harvesting is the birds. Being connoisseurs and gossips, the word soon gets around the bird population that the elderberries are getting ripe. I have scouted a patch intending within a week or so to make a harvest only to find that within the week my competitors have depleted the treasure.

However, once an untouched patch is found, it is an easy task to fill a large pail with berry clusters. I snip them off with scissors into a pail on my belt. This is perhaps the easiest part. The berries then have to be stripped from the stems and bits and pieces of stems and leaves sorted out.

Once you have your berries cleaned, you are on your way to pies, jelly, elderberry juice or wine. Add about a cup of water for each quart of berries. Simmer for ten to fifteen minutes. Mash the berries and continue simmering for another fifteen minutes or so. Strain the mash through a jelly bag and you have the basic ingredient for a fine jelly or a delicious juice. Follow any good recipe for jelly; sweeten to taste for juice. It mixes well with other juices. This product rates high in vitamin C, higher than the citrus fruits.

Another use for the elderberry is based on the pithy stems. Small boys find the pith easy to push out, making for excellent pea shooters, whistles and the like. Early in the maple industry, hollow elderberry stems were used as spiles when the maples were tapped. These have given way to metal spiles. But the small boy in an elderberry patch can arm himself with a fine array of weaponry.

Elderberries are not hard to find. Since they prefer the moist bottom lands along streams, you should look for them along the banks. Get to know the elderberry. Its beauty and tastiness will add a new dimension to your life.

CHAPTER 30

Grandma's Cookies
Chicken Fat

One of many fond memories of my grandmother is her sugar cookies. She was a master at cookie making. She was also famous (in my eyes at least) for her cinnamon buns and her mincemeat tarts, which sustained me at college. But I treasure most the memory of her sugar cookies. They were light, crisp, a delicate pale gold. They melted in your mouth. There never seemed to be enough of them.

Every so often she would announce that it was time to make sugar cookies. It was many years later that I realized what triggered this endeavor. The announcement made, she would get out her ingredients, a large ceramic bowl, spoons and measuring cups, her rolling board and pin, and start. The recipe was in her head. The first decision was how many to make. Again, it was many years before I knew what determined the size of the batch. Six dozen, eight dozen, ten dozen, whatever the number, she began to measure out the ingredients.

With everything mixed up, she came to the crucial part, test cookies. With the oven in the old wood stove at the proper temperature, a test cookie would be produced. If I was around, and I always tried to be, she would ask my opinion. Breaking the cookie in half, we would carefully eat the first test. "Do you think it needs more vanilla?" I might nod yes. "Is it sweet enough?" "Maybe a little more sugar." I would give my opinion. She would ask, "Do you think they are too crisp?" Or "The oven is too hot." Whether she ever took my advice or not, I was never really sure. But after several test bakings she would be satisfied and start the main bake.

Most of the cookies came out thin, crisp, tender and plain. Some had a large seeded raisin in the center. My grandmother used lots of seeded raisins in her baking. Now I seldom find seeded raisins on the grocery shelves. Some featured a walnut or pecan. Around Christmas she decorated with red and green colored sugar. At Valentine's day a delicious pink frosting covered her hearts and cupids. At Halloween, orange pumpkins, and chocolate witches appeared. She had a great collection of cookie cutters. Each holiday had its own shapes. When I was very young the cookies featured all sorts of animals. But my favorite, in later years, was the few she made just for me with caraway seeds thickly sprinkled over the top and baked to a crisp.

Oh, they were delicious. She was always careful not to over bake. The light delicate color of the final product was important. Although I always thought those that occasionally appeared browned were perfectly acceptable. That first bite would melt in your mouth. I used to roll the crumbs around with my tongue while they dissolved, a perfect ambrosia. The aroma of those metal sheets, covered with hot disks, as they were pulled out of the oven was almost overpowering.

When she left us, her recipe left with her. She had never written it down. My gentle wife had discussed cookie making with her a number of times and so tried to duplicate the formula. She used the test cookie technique. The results were good, but something was missing. They did not have that tender crispness. They did not melt in one's mouth as did my grandmother's.

Then one day my wife remembered the secret. It was chicken fat. In looking back, I recall hearing my grandmother say something about "I guess there is enough chicken fat to make cookies again." I am sure it was the amount of chicken fat that determined the size of the batch that she would be making.

We now have the procedure down pat. The process is similar to my grandmother's except that we have a recipe to follow. I contribute, as I did before, by testing the test cookies. In the course of the experimentation another secret was discovered. In order to get that delicious, melt in your mouth crispness, powdered sugar is an important ingredient.

Assemble the following ingredients:

½ cup chicken fat	1 tsp. vanilla
½ cup margarine or butter	1 tsp. almond flavoring
1 cup confectioner's sugar	2½ cups all purpose flour
½ cup granulated sugar	1 tsp. baking powder
2 eggs	1 tsp. salt

1. Cream sugars and shortening.
2. Mix in eggs and flavoring.
3. Measure flour, blend dry ingredients.
4. Stir into egg-shortening mixture.
5. Refrigerate 2-3 hours.
6. Roll out on lightly floured pastry cloth or board, 3/16" thick. Cut in desired shapes.
7. Bake at 375 degrees, 7-8 minutes or until delicately golden.

CHAPTER 31

Yardstick Excalibur

I was very young when I was first introduced to King Arthur and the Knights of the Round Table. The tales were read and reread for me. I spent many happy hours putting the Black Knight over the bank into the river behind my house and performing acts of valor and chivalry. Dragons and princesses benefitted in one way or another from my prowess with the lance and sword. Astride an old sawhorse, with a sapling in hand I rode many a hard mile in defense of justice. A large oatmeal box with alterations became a shining silver helmet.

One winter evening I was sitting in our darkened parlor cross-legged under the parlor table. I was lost in contemplation. A relative asked me to come to him in the adjacent bright living room. For some reason I did not respond to his entreaties. After several attempts he stated that the "Boogey man" would get me if I did not come out. The boogey man was something new to me and I responded.

Up to that point I had roamed our large home without fear and with impunity. The concept of the boogey man had an immediate effect. I became apprehensive of the dark, even of empty rooms. Previously I had, unaided and unaccompanied, negotiated the stairs and the long hall to my bedroom. Suddenly the journey became at best a chore, at worst a somewhat terrifying passage.

My mother immediately realized the problem and tried to point out that during the several years that I had been around no boogey man had ever been known to exist. I acknowledged the fact but the seed had been planted and I was afraid to go upstairs alone. The hallway was a severe hazard. When I reached the head of the stairs I had to negotiate the long hall to turn on the light in my room, return to the head of the stairs to turn out the hall light and renegotiate the now darkened hall to reach the warm glow of my sanctuary. My mother told me years later that on that particular evening she had dressed down the relative so severely that he rarely made visits after that.

The local feed mill distributed numbers of yardsticks on which it had its advertising. We had acquired a supply of these thin strips of wood which were placed in several handy spots around the house. One day after a session with King Arthur I devised a method of defeating the boogey man or anything else that might be lurking about to do me harm.

The yardstick became Excalibur, King Arthur's famous sword. When it came time to ascend the stairs to go to bed, I would turn on the light and with my yardstick firmly clenched in my right hand announce to anything within hearing that I was armed with the famous weapon, Excalibur. I proclaimed that should I be menaced in any manner whatsoever my trusty sword would eliminate the threat in short order.

With the sword deftly swishing back and forth, thrusting and parrying and with the proclamation reiterated at strategic intervals I safely negotiated the route to my bedroom. I would feint, parry, thrust. With my swishing blade I would advance up the stairs, thrusting into dark corners, loudly proclaiming the keenness of my steel. Passing a dark bedroom was no longer a problem.

From then on I had no problems with the dark as long as I had my yardstick Excalibur. Occasionally I would have to carry an arm load of swords back down the stairs to replenish the supply. But other than that minor difficulty the boogey man had been defeated.

As time passed so did the need for Excalibur. Somewhere along the line the boogey man faded into oblivion. But there was a time when he was real and so was King Arthur and so was Excalibur.

So, Arthur Your Majesty, Rex Your Highness, I owe you one.

CHAPTER 32

Flying Squirrel
Night Glider

I have a large number of birdhouses that need annual cleaning and maintenance. This is something I usually do in the late winter or early spring. My garden is still frozen solid. I'm champing at the bit to get at the outdoor chores. So birdhouse cleaning fits in very nicely.

One warm February day I decided it was time to clean the birdhouses. There was quite a bit of snow on the ground but it was pleasant and sunny. Most of my birdhouses are constructed to facilitate cleaning with a side or bottom that can easily be unfastened and removed.

As I approached a particular birdhouse fashioned from a piece of log and attached to the trunk of a black cherry, I noticed that the entrance was plugged with a mass of shredded bark. This was not the first time that this had happened and I was pretty sure of its occupant. For occupied it was. Occasionally after the birds have abandoned their birdhouses the flying squirrels move in. Over the years I have disturbed a number of flying squirrels when cleaning my birdhouses and so have learned the shredded bark signal.

84

The 'Tenant'

I passed up cleaning this particular birdhouse. Each day I would inspect it as closely as possible without disturbing the tenant. Sometimes the entrance would be completely blocked, sometimes partly open. Several times as I observed the open entrance it would become blocked. The occupant was closing the door. Sometimes I could see eyes peering out at me. This particular animal occupied the house throughout the following summer. Whether young were raised or not I could not tell.

The adult flying squirrel is perhaps nine inches in length with a tail of an additional four inches. The most striking physical appearance of the resting animal is the very large black eyes. The head seems all eyes as the bundle of fur peers out its den hole at me. The large eyes indicate that this animal is nocturnal. I've never seen one out in broad daylight except for those I've disturbed. The fur is usually a fawn brown with white underneath. Many I've seen seem to be more grey, a ghost grey.

Cherry Pits

Litters of three to six young are produced once each year, probably during the last of April. Their food consists of leaves, buds, fruits, nuts, bark, seeds and many insects. The houses I clean will be filled and the ground below covered with halves of black cherry pits. Black cherry pits seem to be a winter staple for my squirrels. In the wild, our North Country flying squirrels (probably Sciurpterus volans) use abandoned woodpecker holes as nesting sites. One writer states to the effect that where there are no woodpeckers there are no flying squirrels.

The most interesting aspect of these shy little animals is their flying which of course is not flying but gliding. There is a double flap of skin called the patagium starting at each side of the neck, extending to the wrists and thence to the ankles. When the four legs are extended outward the patagium forms a surface not unlike an airfoil. When not in use the patagium folds and is held close to the body becoming inconspicuous.

Once launched the flying squirrel has considerable control. It can bank and turn to avoid obstacles, tree branches and the like. The launch is usually from high in a tree and terminates lower on the trunk of a nearby tree. On landing the body turns sharply upward so that it is nearly vertical. The four limbs are thrown out toward the landing site producing a parachute-like

85

form which has a braking effect on the air speed. This allows the animal to land gently in such a position as to be able to scamper up or down the trunk should a predator be near. One writer says that in flight the head is lowered making the leading edge of the patagium curve downward producing an even more effective and efficient airfoil.

I have not been very successful in observing these nocturnal flights. I occasionally see a swoop in the car headlights as I return late in the evening. Flying squirrels that I have disturbed in their nests have never taken to the air. They scamper up the tree trunk and hide until I have gone.

Flying squirrels are much more abundant than most of us realize. Their nocturnal habits and their natural shyness keep us from noticing them. If you have access to a wooded area where there are nesting sites and adequate food, vigilance will reward you with an acquaintance of this timid North Country resident.

CHAPTER 33

Orange Crates
A Lost Treasure

Some years ago I was working with two of my offspring. We needed a small section of thin lumber. None was available so I had to saw out a piece. During the operation I remarked that "I wish we had an orange crate." "What's an orange crate?" one of them asked.

It was at that moment that I realized the horrendous fact that the orange crate had become extinct. This exceptionally useful item, a plaything, source of building materials, inspiration for all sorts of furniture and household items had disappeared without my realizing it. It had become an artifact.

Saturday, beginning when I was about nine or ten, I would go to the local grocery to see if any orange crates had been emptied. Usually the empty crates, along with other wooden boxes, would have been thrown out where, sometime later, whatever had not been scavanged would be burned. If luck was with me there might be an orange crate along with a wooden box or two. These were quickly and carefully spirited home. There was demand for these items and I did not want to be conspicuous with my acquisitions.

"What's an orange crate?" my offspring asked again. I described the double compartment box. Two ends and the middle divider were made of ¾ inch boards about 14"x14". These were fastened together with six quarter inch boards about 4"x36". One end of the crate sported a 12"x12" colored poster advertising the company. If one was careful one could salvage all of the lumber together with a small handful of nails.

My offspring were not impressed. "What is so wonderful about an orange crate?" was the rejoinder. My description had become rather eloquent. They had sensed a note of excitement creeping into my voice. I pointed out that when I was young the orange crate had been my only source of building materials. The thin boards were appropriate for my limited tool collection.

87

I described how simple chairs could be constructed using just a saw. I described, how, with a few extra boards, several orange crates could become a castle or a fort, the next day a schooner plowing the high seas or a snug pirate's cave on a desert island.

I had stimulated their interest. "Did you get them for free?" one asked. I replied that much of the food arrived at the grocery in wooden boxes that were usually discarded. During the depression inspired orange crate users became widespread. Articles appeared in the newspapers and magazines describing new uses for orange crates. Books were published. "Place two boards across the top of two orange crates standing on end. Cover with curtains and you have a vanity," was one I distinctly remember because I was asked to contribute two of my precious crates for that useless project.

I described how a series of orange crates nailed to the wall became a sturdy set of shelving for household items or library books. A coat of paint and an orange crate became a bedside stand and a useful companion for many years. The uses came flooding back and I went on and on.

A week or two later, digging around upstairs in the old barn, we found two orange crates with end posters intact, "ULTRA brand from Ultra, California," COLD WIND, Fullerton, California (no zip code). I described how I had, with my hand jig saw, cut the end piece with its poster into a jig saw puzzle. By slanting the cuts in various directions through the ¾ inch board, the puzzle was made rather difficult. Along with the orange crate we dredged up some book ends, shoe racks, test tube racks (for my first chemistry set), a bird house and several other items that had metamorphosed from the priceless orange crate. My progeny were impressed.

Bursting with pleasant nostalgia I was transported back to when a happy Saturday meant my old tools and an orange crate. Filled with sadness I was distressed that my offspring would never experience this pleasure. Modern technology and progress have created a loss that cannot be filled. This was confirmed when they both, wistfully, and almost in unison said, "I wish we had orange crates."

CHAPTER 34

JOHN NORTON

Jumping Mouse
Kangaroos in the North Country

Several years ago I had a severe problem with my strawberries. Each time I inspected the patch I'd find a few half-ripe berries in the paths. Sometimes a bite would have been taken out of the ripe side. Each day more and more berries appeared. Now they were lined up in neat rows. My irritation became fury as this continued day after day, greatly depleting my potential harvest. I watched from a distance and soon spied the culprit. It was a chipmunk.

I have a live animal trap so I reasoned that I'd catch the offender and solve the problem. Within a half hour after setting the trap my sunflower seeds as bait had him trapped. So it was into the car and down the road a mile or so to a patch of woods where I freed the troublemaker. Where there is one chipmunk there probably are two so I reset the trap and soon had another. That day I made four trips down the road. Before the strawberry season ended I had made about thirty trips. I knew we had chipmunks but was totally unaware that we had a horde of chipmunks.

Each spring I start my routine. I now have a holding cage in which I can put several of the little beasties thus avoiding the large number of trips down the road. The price of gasoline has begun to make my strawberries somewhat costly.

New Character

One morning, not long ago, I went out to inspect the trap. The trap was sprung but from a distance I could see nothing. Closer examination showed that I did have an animal, but not a chipmunk. I lifted the trap to inspect this furry little bundle.

The first thing that struck me was the extremely long tail that was two and a half to three times longer than the tiny body. The rear legs were long and folded under the body. This gentle little animal looked at me from within the trap then took a few short hops. That was the giveaway. I knew I had caught an Eastern Jumping Mouse.

I looked the quarry over carefully. It was really a beautiful animal. The sides were a brownish gold, blending to almost black on the top. The huddled body seemed to be less than two inches long. With its bright eyes, tiny ears, twitching whiskers, busy forepaws and those elongated rear legs, it probably didn't weigh an ounce. When it hopped around the trap-cage there was that peculiar kangaroo-like gait.

I've seen them several times in the field, brief glimpses of a slim, bounding bullet, racing through the grass. Once in the early spring when digging a load of gravel for my drive, I unearthed a tight, furry ball of sleeping life. It proved to be a hibernating jumping mouse, one of the very few true hibernators we have in the North Country.

I did not want to break its hibernation, as the weather was still harsh, so I carefully placed it in a protected place surrounded by its nesting materials to await more favorable conditions. In about three weeks it was gone.

This mouse is probably Zapus Hudsonius. It ranges from New England all the way up to Manitoba. It will produce 2 to 3 litters per year with 2 to 4 young per litter. The diet is largely seeds with berries and beech nuts in season.

I took the trap in to show my family and then out to let its resident go. I wanted to see its movements as well as possible, so I picked some low cover. I opened one door of the trap. He hopped to the edge, took one look around and leaped to the ground, a prodigious leap out on to the forest floor. His leap was about the equivalent of a six foot man leaping half a football field.

I watched as he stayed motionless, blending into the background, a beautiful camouflage. One slow, careful step toward him and he was away. Three or four leaps and he was out twenty feet and lost to sight. Kangaroos in the North Country? Well, no, but the adaptation is here.

The next time when you are in the field and a tiny bundle of life bounces away through the tall grass, you'll know that you have see the nearest thing we have to a kangaroo.

JOHN NORTON

Great Horned Owl
Majestic Predator

One dusk, in my early teens, while fishing on the Black River, I spied a large bird in a tall tree on the river bank. I did not know the bird and allowed my boat to drift down toward his perch. I could see that it was an owl.

As I watched it, it watched me and at the approach of the boat, launched itself into the tall nearby trees. With absolute silence and dangling feet, it deftly maneuvered its way through the thick growth. The massive wingspread, easily five feet, would seem to be a deterrent to forest flight. But as I watched, it adroitly and swiftly made its way through the tree tops with ease.

Later, at home with the bird book, I decided that I had been watching a Great Horned Owl, although I was not close enough to see the feather tufts that give it its name. Every time since, when I have been fortunate to watch one fly, I marvel at the ease with which it threads its way through some forest tangle.

It has many other names, Great Hoot Owl being very common. In some areas it is called Cat Owl because of the cat-like cries it sometimes produces. Its usual song is a series of five hoots with the second and third hoots coming close together. Once you learn the "hooo hoot-hoot hooo hooo", identification is unmistakable. At night the call carries well and if you listen you will probably find that it is a resident somewhere within your area.

The Great Horned Owl (Bubo Virginianus), a large bird probably two feet in length, is not much of a nest builder. Most of the time it uses abandoned crow or hawk nests. In a contest with a hawk for a nest, the Great Horned Owl is usually triumphant. When forced to construct its own nest, the results are less than truimphant.

Stair-Step Family

Two eggs comprise the usual clutch, but up to five have been observed. Usually these are laid some days apart but incubation starts immediately. This results in a stair-step family with chicks of different ages and development occupying the same domicile.

Egg laying can begin as early as January but it is more likely that February or early March is the preferred time. This means that incubation is an immediate and continuous process as the eggs would freeze if left uncovered for even a short period. I have seen photographs of an incubating owl covered with freshly fallen snow, placidly protecting and warming the clutch beneath her in the poorly insulated nest.

The Great Horned Owl feasts on almost anything that moves that is not too large to handle. It is a vicious and efficient predator on insects, rats, snakes, birds, mice, rabbits and fish. Some time after the owl has dined, the undigested parts of its meal (bones, hair, feathers) are egested in the form of pellets.

93

Analysis of these pellets provides the ornithologist with a fine record of its menu.

Apparently it does not have a very acute sense of smell, or it is not discriminating, as it frequently dines on skunks. In areas where the skunk population is high, the Great Horned owl (Bubo) population is apt to be high. I recall the look on a local taxidermist's face as he showed me a reeking, skunk fed, carcass of a large great horned owl. His words were crisp and blue as he opined about the ancestry of his customer.

For some reason crows and owls do not mix. Crows take great delight in harassing owls. Although the owl could easily dispatch a crow, it seems to tolerate the abuse with stoic indifference. Owl decoys are used with great success on crows. The normally wiley crow loses his head, so to speak, and will continue to harass a decoy even though the hunter reveals himself. An owl household nearby was frequently the object of crow invective. Sometimes when I would hear the abusive language, I could walk slowly into the edge of the milling raucous flock before the crows would break off the engagement.

For many years it has been my habit to arise early each morning to go over the day's work. During the weeks of early winter, this meant arising in total darkness. A pair of Great Horned Owls occupied a nest in some pines in a corner of my woods.

In the early weeks of winter they would be returning from the night's hunt about the time I was studying for the day's work. Almost every day, until the egg laying started, I would first hear them in the distance as they started their return. One would give the call. The other would respond. An interval would pass with the calls then repeated somewhat nearer. They followed a definite route in their return which led right past the study where I was working. Frequently there would be an overlap, one answering before the other was finished.

There was enough difference in the pitch of their notes that they produced fine two-noted chords for my enjoyment. Sometimes they halted in some large pines nearby to give me a last morning serenade.

I enjoyed these serenades for several winter seasons. Then one spring I discovered a huge bundle of feathers in some brush. It appeared that someone had shot one of my birds. The survivor apparently left the area (or also was shot) as I have heard no more early morning winter performances. Nor have I seen this majestic bird threading its way through my woods.

CHAPTER 36

©1984
JOHN MCRION

Shrew
Tiny Powerhouse

One warm, drizzly day during the deer hunting season several years ago, I decided to just sit. It was too warm to do much moving around dressed as I was. I would get wet if I took off enough clothing to be comfortable. So I picked a nice cozy spot under a hemlock where I could watch over a small valley. I was under cover. The rain had a lulling effect. The duff on which I was sitting was soft, comfortable and dry. It was a pleasant situation. As I scanned the valley for deer signs, not too optimistically, I caught a slight movement out of the corner of my eye. I shifted my gaze to the duff but saw nothing. A moment later there was another movement. This time I saw it, a shrew. Then off to another side there was a flash of movement and there was another of these tiny powerhouses. In all, I saw at least three separate shrews. Previously, besides preserved specimens in the laboratory, I'd had but an occasional glimpse.

There is a rule in zoology that says the smaller the mammal the faster its engine must run. As an animal increases in size, its volume increases much faster than does its surface area. This means that the larger the animal is, the less heat it will lose per unit body weight. It has relatively less surface area through which to lose heat. Thus it does not have to run its engine as fast to make up the heat loss.

The elephant has a heart rate around twenty. Man's heart rate is around eighty. The shrew has a rate of several hundred beats per minute. This tiny motor races at this very high rate all through its existence. It literally burns itself up. To fuel this tiny body it must eat at least its own weight each day. When activity is high it probably doubles that amount. Any engine that is raced constantly does not last long. The life span of the shrew is one and a half to two and a half years. During that time several litters of three to nine offspring will be produced.

While it is classed as an insectivore, it will eat almost anything edible, insects, worms, snails, seeds. Since it burns its fuel rapidly it must refuel frequently, at least every hour or so. Shrews are not gregarious. They tend toward the solitary, except at mating time. If you put two shrews in a cage, in all probability you will soon have one inside the other. A shrew will attack, kill and eat a mouse, an animal that may be 30-50 times its own size. Its appetite is insatiable.

The shrew is unique in the mammalian class in that it is the only mammal that secretes a venom. This apparently works on the nervous system of its prey subduing it in a relatively short time. Its bite can cause pain in the human for several days.

So here I had a shrew, probably the short-tailed shrew (Blaria brevicauda). Actually it is quite common in woodlands, but rarely seen because of its size and the habit of working beneath the forest duff. I forgot my deer hunting and concentrated on the activities before me. Their movement was incessant. The very pointed nose was constantly probing into and under the leaves and other debris on the forest floor. These little mites would disappear under the duff to reappear almost immediately some distance away.

The tiny eyes and ears I could not see. In their searching, they rarely came close to one another. When it seemed as though there might be a confrontation each would turn aside. Did they recognize that a showdown might be fatal? Nothing escaped their attention. Every nook and cranny was probed. These little animals were about two and a half inches long with a tail that was probably less than an inch. I stretched my leg and they were gone.

96

If you want to see Northern New York's most ravenous creature, our most racy engine, you will have to sit quietly on the forest floor, let patience be your guide and hope for a fair amount of luck.

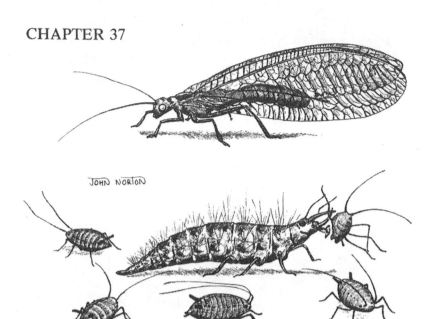

CHAPTER 37

JOHN NORTON

Lacewing
The Golden Eyed Fly

Along about twilight, as I walk through the tall grass or even as I sit in a lawn chair at the edge of my garden, I begin to see the Lacewing. This is an animal with which every gardener should be familiar and in love. The Lacewing can be found almost anywhere in the United States and Southern Canada. So there is no excuse for not knowing him.

A pale green fluttering moves out as my walk disturbs, awakens him from the long daylight siesta. After resting through most of the day the Lacewing is eager to feed. Two pairs of delicate green wings account for the name. A pair of brilliant golden eyes are responsible for another name, the "Golden-eyed fly." The diaphanous, pastel green wings folded in an "A" frame over its body combine with the arresting golden eyes to make a beautiful sight. But it is not only the beauty of this insect that should attract and interest the gardener.

Aphids, plant lice, can be the bane of anyone trying to grow almost anything. These tiny sucking insects that mulitply with abandon can literally suck the life out of a plant overnight. Were it not for some aphis predators like the ladybird beetle and the lacewing, aphids would overrun our gardens.

When she is ready to deposit her eggs, the female lacewing usually finds a herd of aphids. She usually lays her egg clusters within or near the herd but she does it in a rather unusual way.

Each egg is cemented to a slender strand projecting well above the leaf or plant stalk that forms the aphis pasture. The reason for this seems to be to keep the hatching egg up and out of the way of possible predators.

Ants that sometimes shepherd aphids might consume the eggs if they were within the herd. But swaying above the surface like some exotic plant growth, they are usually unnoticed. Actually, predator protection is only a partial reason for this unusual egg deposition. A major danger to the eggs is from the hatching larva themselves. Were the eggs to be deposited in clusters on the surface, as is usual with many insects, the first emerging larva would consume unhatched eggs and subsequent hatchlings.

It is these rather lizard-like larva that should gain our attention as garden lovers. These larva are voracious feeders of aphids. So all consuming in their passion for ingesting the plant lice that they are called aphis lions.

In full gear and in the midst of a good supply of aphids, the aphis lion can consume an aphid a minute. Using its curved and grooved jaws it impales an aphid. Then holding the aphid up, it allows the victim's juices to drain down the grooves into its mouth. Once the container is empty it is discarded and another aphid impaled. This goes on for 6 to 10 days depending on temperature, humidity and the supply of aphids.

After about a week, a glistening pea-sized cocoon is formed on the underside of a leaf and the process of metamorphosis begins. After about two more weeks of development, the adult emerges and the cycle is complete. The adults also are great consumers of aphids. But their appetites pale next to their larva. Nevertheless, they will spend most of the hours of darkness scouring plant life for aphids to consume and for egg deposition locations.

Many insects winter over as eggs or metamorphosing larva. All insect activity is dependent on temperature. When the temperature drops, activity drops. This is not necessarily the case with the lacewing. It can be quite active at temperatures well below freezing. It can withstand the rigors of winter and emerge in the spring ready for business.

This beautiful, delicate, glistening, green-winged, golden-eyed beauty is unique in yet another fashion. It might be described as the skunk of the insect world, for when captured, it emits a disagreeable odor which is difficult to get rid of.

So here we have a fairly common, widespread animal that has a rather unusual life style. It follows usual insect patterns to a considerable extent, but also deviates. It is a beautiful jewel in the grass and a skunk as well. It is the gardener's friend, the aphids' enemy. If you grow plants, you should cultivate the Lacewing.

CHAPTER 38

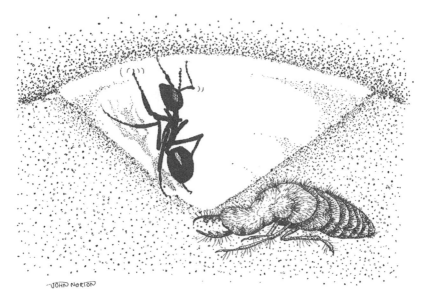

JOHN NORTON

Ant Lion
Trapper

It is the larval form of the ant lion that I find most interesting. The adult resembles the lacewing, or better, the damselfly. This family Myrmeleontidae has representatives around the world. I have no idea what species I have observed. The larva is a vicious ugly creature. It appears to be able to move only backward. It has formidable elongated jaws and lives at the bottom of a conical pit carefully dug in sand.

The pit is constructed by placing grains of sand on its head and flipping them outward. Gradually the insect flips out sand until a cone trap has been constructed. The predator buries itself at the bottom of this cone with just its jaws protruding and waits.

If an ant or other unsuspecting insect should blunder into the trap, grains of sand will cascade to the bottom. The slope of the sides is such that the sand grains are lightly held in place. Sometimes the slope is so fragile that the ant tumbles immediately to the bottom. Once within the grasp of the fierce and efficient jaws, the struggling ant is pulled beneath the sand. After consuming his dinner the ant lion repairs the trap and again settles down to wait.

101

Should the victim not cascade down immediately but appear to be making an escape, the lion will shower it with a buck shot pattern of sand from the bottom. This makes the sides of the cone more likely to slide down and also confuses and dislodges the intended meal. Usually a short bombardment will bring the victim within reach.

This type of nutrition is pretty chancy. If ants are not plentiful in the neighborhood, meals may be few and far between. But the trigger on this trap does not seem to mind. The ant lion can go for many weeks without feeding. There also seems to be evidence that some species of ant lions produce an ant-like scent to further enhance their traps.

One time when my offspring were young, I chanced on a colony of ant lions not too far from our home. Of necessity it was in a spot where the sand was protected and dry. Wet sand does not tumble well. About twenty cones pocked the surface of the ground. When they first caught my eye I dropped an ant into a trap or two to test the efficacy. Sure enough the ants disappeared almost immediately.

I took my offspring to the spot and pointed out the structures. We then spent many minutes gathering ants and other small insects to tempt the trap triggers. During the following weeks my offspring visited the trap regularly, fascinated by the precise construction and operation of the little cones. I expect we harbored the best fed colony of ant lions in the county.

Nature is replete with fascinating methods of obtaining food. Each animal seems unique in some way. Each species has its own unusual method of satisfying its nutritional needs. The ant lion demonstrates this diversity. We are part of a marvelous world. The more we learn about it, the more amazing it becomes. I feel that as part of this world we have an obligation to learn about it, to understand it and most of all, to preserve it.

CHAPTER 39

JOHN NORTON

Whip-poor-will
Night Warbler

Although I am sure I had heard its call before, my earliest recollection of the Whip-poor-will was on a camping trip when I was about twelve. We were established on the shore of a clear Adirondack Lake. Supper was over, the dishes washed. Everything was shipshape for the night. The camp fire glowed. We sat in silence thinking of the trout we had missed that day and of the trout we would outwit tomorrow. From back in the woods a Whip-poor-will gave the first announcement of twilight. It was answered by one closer by. Another confirmed the event. Suddenly a Whip-poor-will that was almost within our campsite joined the chorus. We were startled, not only by the nearness and thus the loudness of the sound, but by how different it was when its origin was almost within one's ear.

We remained silent, listening, until a shower of sparks from the camp fire sent the bird off into the darkness. Whenever I hear a Whip-poor-will I instantly smell the cool clean air of that mountain lake. I see the dying camp fire. I sense the pleasant satisfaction of a day well spent, the coming of a night well provided for. I have a feeling, momentarily at least, that all is right with my world.

The Whip-poor-will belongs to a group of birds called the goatsuckers, whose common characteristics are big mouths and weak feet. Our Eastern Whip-poor-will (Caprimulgus vociferus) is a widely known bird because of its call, but a rarely seen bird because of its drab garb and nocturnal ways.

About nine to ten inches in length, this "dead leaf" colored bird is a ground nester. In fact, it can hardly be said to nest at all. No nest is constructed. A pair of eggs is laid in leaves on the ground in deep wood thickets. When a parent is incubating these eggs, the camouflage is superb. When the parents are away from the nest, a leaf or two does the same trick. If disturbed, the bird usually flies a short distance settling back to the ground to become once again invisible. The flight is silent. If white tail feathers are observed, you have seen a male. If the bird is on the nest and is disturbed, it will play the crippled grouse trick. The charade is different, if not better, than that of the grouse in that the Whip-poor-will gasps and thrashes around as though mortally wounded.

The primary food is insects taken in a noiseless flight. The feeding begins about sundown and continues sporadically throughout the night. The bill is short but the mouth opens wide. The upper part of the bill features a number of long stiff bristly feathers which function to enlarge the mouth like a funnel. This is a great aid in capturing and swallowing insects. The feeding is interrupted by periods of song, some of which can be lengthy. As dawn approaches the urge to sing subsides and the birds drop to the ground for a day of sleep.

The Whip-poor-will is migratory, breeding in Canada, Manitoba to Nova Scotia and south to Louisiana and Georgia. It winters along the Gulf. Probably the easiest way to see Whip-poor-wills is by car. Well after dark, traverse the back woods roads. A bright red reflection from the eyes in a sandy patch in the road tells you that a Whip-poor-will is there, probably dusting itself. If you can ease the car up slowly, you can frequently get quite close for a good view in the head lights.

Years ago, when I first moved to my present home location, there were Whip-poor-wills singing in my woods. One May morning about two o'clock a bird started singing in a pine just outside my bedroom window. I listened with considerable pleasure to the bird just a few feet away. After about ten minutes, I began to weary of the serenade. After a half an hour of almost continuous singing, I began to feel some irritation. After an hour of almost uninterrupted raucous noise, I went to the window and in strong, loud language advised the bird to depart and never come back. I assume the word got around that the clearing was now occupied by an inconsiderate, tone deaf, curmudgeon, as never in the nearly twenty-five years since has one attempted to broadcast from that perch.

CHAPTER 40

Bufo
Bufo the Smart

Bufo was a large one, probably the largest in Lewis County. He was large probably because he was smart. He was large probably because he had the best food supply in Lewis County because he was smart.

Several years ago we purchased one of those ultraviolet insect traps. I really wanted it to clear out all the mosquitoes so that at any time of the day or night I could walk around or sit outdoors without being irritated by mosquitoes. In theory, the ultraviolet was to provide an irresistible luring effect to bring insects in so that they would touch a series of electrodes and thus do themselves in. Oh, it worked. Turn it on at night and you would soon begin to hear sharp snaps as unsuspecting marauders brushed against the inner hot grid, made contact and spiraled to the ground. During the day it was largely ineffective.

There were two other things wrong with the trap. The area in its vicinity would get rather messy with the carcasses of its victims and it didn't keep the area free from mosquitoes. To be sure, it did garner some mosquitoes but it proved most effective against all sorts of moths. Moths don't sting. They are relatively innocuous, at least as far as my personal comfort is concerned. To effectively trap the day and night flying mosquito over the entire yard I suspect that the ultraviolet source would have to be so intense that one would get an instant tan at 100 feet. We experimented with locating the trap and finally settled on a nail just inside the garage. The concrete floor of the garage would facilitate sweeping up the evening's debris. For a while we were reasonably satisfied with the arrangement. Granted, the yard was not free from mosquitoes, but then all of life is a compromise. The trap was better than nothing.

Each morning I would go out with dustpan and broom in hand and sweep up the carnage of the night before. I would self satisfiedly dump the remains in the compost pit and go about the day's business. After about a week, I began to notice that the night's take was getting smaller and smaller. Observing the trap confirmed that it was as effective as ever. All evening we would hear its snap, crackle and pop as it did its deadly work. But in the morning there were few if any bodies on the floor.

The answer seemed to be that something was eating our take. I first suspected mice, since we have a colony of deermice that come in occasionally from the field to raid our dog food cache. But we saw no mice. What we did see was Bufo. At first we called him Bufo the Magnificent because he certainly was a magnificent animal.

Bufo was a common toad (Bufo americanus), common but also uncommon because of his size and of course, his intelligence. Continued observation determined the following pattern. Shortly after we would turn on the light, Bufo would appear. We never did learn the location of his daytime home. He would take a stance, out of the direct ultraviolet light, in the shadow, directly under the trap-light. As dead and dying insects slowly drifted down, Bufo would flip out his efficient tongue and harvest them. He would remain in place, within the circle, for whatever period we left the light on. I experimented with turning it off and then

106

back on at a later time. Sometimes he would reappear, some-times, not. Perhaps he had been satiated. Perhaps he had turned elsewhere for his hunting.

For Bufo, the result of all this was that he grew larger and fatter. By the end of the first summer he would have taken first prize in any toad beauty contest. I was apprehensive when I put the trap away in the fall. I wanted to insure that he would return in the spring. I toyed with the idea of capturing and keeping him in the cellar over the winter, but finally thought better of it.

The snows came, three feet in the woods nearby, four feet eventually on our lawn and enormous mounds where it slid off the roofs. As spring approached I began to get things ready for the reawakening. I took down the trap for a cleaning, wondering if Bufo would reappear.

The end of May arrived. The toad breeding season was past. The bug season was upon us in force and I put out the trap. Each morning I swept up the debris and threw it on the compost heap. Apparently Bufo was not going to appear. I wondered if he had survived the winter and had found another feeding spot, or had he not made it through the cold in his underground bed? Then one morning I went to sweep the garage floor and found it clean. "Bufo's back" I announced, confident that this magic was my toad. Sure enough, the next evening, shortly after I turned on the light, Bufo appeared. He positioned himself, out of the direct ultraviolet light (Did he know it was bad for his eyes?), in the shadow, directly under the trap light and as the dead and dying insects drifted down, he flipped out his efficient tongue and dined.

Bufo the Smart in all his magnificence was back.

CHAPTER 41

JOHN NORTON

Juneberries
Unknown and Underrated

Several years ago, while blueberrying on Tug Hill, a daughter harvested a pail of Juneberries while the rest of us concentrated on the blueberries. That evening after the last of the blueberries had been cleaned and stashed away in the freezer, we feasted on a hot Juneberry pie, a fabulous reward for the hot day of stooping over the endless blueberry tangle.

What is the Juneberry? It is one of the most underrated and neglected North Country fruits. It goes by many names, Shad, Shadbush, Shadberry, Shadblow, Serviceberry, Billberry, and Juneberry. The scientific name is Amelanchier canadensis. Of the several Amelanchier species, a canadensis is probably most likely to be found in the North Country and has the most delectable fruit.

You may find this much underrated plant growing as a tree up to 40 feet in height and with a trunk a foot or more in diameter. You are more likely to find it as a shrub with a slender stem. It flowers early in the spring. Many delicate, five-petaled blossoms make it stand out in the woods or in fence rows scattered around pastures. This is the time to locate and mark for reference a supply for the June-July harvest.

Heat Value

The shad is an attractive plant. It seems to have little commercial value although it has the highest heat value of any of our hardwoods. The simple, alternate leaves resemble the maple. The leaf shape is oval with edges that are finely toothed. The bark is very smooth and greyish brown in color. Sometimes it resembles the blue beech. As the tree ages, darker streaks run lengthwise up and down the trunk.

The best part of the Serviceberry is the fruit. Sometime in June or July the clusters of reddish fruit will begin to take on a purple hue. They are now ready. They are difficult to pick, since as many will go into your mouth as into your pail. But if your source is ample and if you persist, you will havest a most delectable reward.

A fond memory of the Juneberry involves the old swimming hole. Our walk back followed an old dirt country road. In an abandoned pasture beside the road, were several Juneberry shrubs. The lack of competition allowed them to grow low and bushy and to produce copious amounts of delicious berries. Each day after an afternoon of swimming, we would stop and gather handfuls of juicy sweet berries. The successive ripening process would provide us with more berries for the following day.

A Fine Resource

The Indians were well aware of the value of the Juneberry. The early colonists also made use of this bountiful delicacy. But somehow, we have grown to overlook a fine resource. It can be used in many of the ways that one uses blueberries. They are fine sprinkled on your cereal. They can be stewed with sugar or honey to provide a delicious sauce. When some of the stewed berries are folded into your muffin batter, a princely product results. Juneberries can be dried, as the Indians and colonists did, or canned or frozen.

Other than eating them out of hand right from the tree, my favorite is the Juneberry pie. Make a crust using your usual recipe. Mix together four cups of berries, one cup of sugar, ¼ cup of flour, two tablespoons of lemon juice and a dash of salt.

Line the tin with crust and fill with this mixture. Cover with the remaining crust. Make a few slashes in the top and bake in a 400 degree oven for about 45 minutes. This results in a superb fruit pie that has a slight taste of almond. It is absolutely delicious hot out of the oven, so time your baking with that in mind.

If you've never crammed a handful of juicy shadberries into your mouth, if you've never spooned billberry sauce over your ice cream, if you've never savored hot serviceberry pie, you've a great treat in store. Get to know this neglected North Country treasure.

CHAPTER 42

JOHN NORTON

Snowshoe Rabbit
The White Ghost

I've had a long and pleasant association with the white ghost, Lepus americanus, or the snowshoe rabbit or varying hare. He goes by many other names. I've spent many happy hours in his close company, sometimes much closer than I realized at the moment.

The varying hare is so-called because he changes his summer brown coat to winter white and back again as the seasons change. He has other adaptations that superbly fit him for winters in the North Country. Locally known as the snowshoe rabbit, the white ghost equips himself with just that. Large feet with stiff hairs between the toes enable him to snowshoe on top of the light fluffy snow when the hound behind is wallowing belly deep trying to keep up.

111

The fur is light but thick, giving fine protection against the cold. As rabbits and hares go, the snowshoe is medium in size, ranging from three to four pounds in weight. In the winter when I am most acquainted with him, his coat is completely white except for black at the tips of the ears.

Lepus knows that his camouflage is good. He will hold as you move by. Many times I have seen where a snowshoe rabbit has come out of his hiding place a foot or two from my snowshoe tracks after I had gone by.

One time I followed a fresh track to where it disappeared into a little bower under the trunk of a fallen tree. There was no track leading out so I knew the animal must still be there, but I could not see it. Quietly I moved forward, intently watching for the sudden flight, carefully scrutinizing the cover for the quarry. I could see nothing. For several minutes I peered through the branches with no results. At last a twitch of the black-tipped ears gave him away, he had been in relatively plain sight a few feet away all the time. Impressed with this camouflage, I quietly backed away leaving the white ghost for another day.

The snowshoe rabbit does not have a den or warren as such. Any accommodating shelter is used and easily abandoned. The young precocious hares are born fully furred and with open eyes. The female makes no nest, often dropping them on a well trod path. They are able to move well shortly after birth.

The gestation period is thirty-six days with the first litter being produced in March. A second litter is normally produced before summer ends. The varying hare population is subject to great cyclic highs and lows. For several years there may be a hare beneath every bush. Succeeding years finds them few and far between. This cyclic variation is closely allied with the numbers of its chief predators, the bobcat, the fox and fisher, and the owl and hawk.

There is strong evidence that the cyclic color changes are triggered by light. When experimental animals are subjected to varying light cycles in the laboratory, their color molts adjust to the artificial seasons independently of temperature or other weather conditions. Hares in the experiment that were masked, so that light did not reach the eyes, did not respond, indicating that the eye must be involved.

During the summer months the snowshoe eats many greens including clover and various grasses. When these are no longer available during the winter months, he feeds on buds and twigs or a number of deciduous trees as well as evergreens.

112

Lepus's range is Northeastern United States running south along the Appalachian chain, Northern Michigan and Wisconsin and Southern Canada. He likes brushy areas surrounded with evergreens. Alder swamps are a favorite habitat. During the peak of the population cycle he spills over into many other habitats.

The numbers at the peak of the cycle are sometimes incredible. A number of years ago during such a peak, we experienced a very warm thaw during a February when there had not been much snow. With the ground bare, the white ghost stood out like a sore thumb. I was astounded one afternoon when I visited a favorite swamp to see the snowshoe everywhere. He crouched low as I passed, probably believing that "freezing" in place would work as well as before. But I spotted him. At one place I counted eight varying hares all within view in the alder thicket. The next week, after a good snowfall, I failed to see a single hare until my dog gave me some help.

Probably the most enjoyment I get from the white ghost is in conjunction with my dog. Once my dog has announced that he is in pursuit, I settle back to read his reports as they come in. If you know your dog, he will constantly advise you of the progress of the chase. Excited yelping will inform you that he has glimpsed the quarry. A mournful bark or two will let you know that he has temporarily lost the trail. As the hare circles, getting close to your ambush, the dog will advise you that a confrontation is imminent.

When I miss seeing the ghost, I do not announce it to the dog. I quietly await the next circle hoping that my dog did not realize my carelessness. If I miss a shot, he is momentarily testy but forgiving as a new set of hot tracks is discovered. He has trouble understanding when I take only a pair of hares, especially when there appear to be many more available. But two snowshoes are enough for a good pot of hasenfeffer and we want to come back another day.

CHAPTER 43

PITCHER PLANT

SINGLE
LEAF

ROSETTE OF LEAVES
SHOWING AN INSECT
TRAPPED IN THE PLANT'S
DIGESTIVE JUICES

SUNDEW

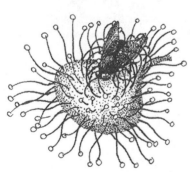

FLY TRAPPED
BY TENTACLES
OF A LEAF

ROSETTE OF
LEAVES

©1984 JOHN NORTON

Carnivorous Plants
They Like Their Meat Too

While our North Country carnivorous plants are not as terrifying or dramatic as those found in science fiction movies, they, nevertheless, are rather spectacular and ingenious in their own way. None of the world's carnivorous plants have long tentacles or collapsing leaves that can capture man or other large animals. Rather, the game that the carnivorous plants stalk is less spectacular, but nevertheless elusive, and its capture requires some rather fascinating adaptations.

I am fortunate to have a part interest in a quaking bog. Over the years, the centuries, a twisted tangle of roots and stems has spread outward from shore and converted a substantial part of the small pond into an undulating, floating carpet. Though I've walked out on it many times, I still have trepidations. I know that there are holes through which I may sink. I know if I stay in one spot for any length of time, the water will creep up around my ankles, sometimes my knees. I am never altogether at home on this shivering platform. But I must make periodic rounds and inspect those peculiar plants that grow on my bog. Among these are the carnivorous plants, the pitcher plant and the sundew.

More precisely, they should be called insectivorous plants since it is mainly the insect on which they feed. The acid conditions in the bog prevent bog dwellers from utilizing any nitrogen that may be present. So the bog dwellers have turned to other sources for their nitrogen requirement. The digested bodies of captured insects provide this nitrogen, as well as other nutrients.

Our North Country pitcher plant (Sarracenia purpurea) is one of several species that inhabit the United States. It is stemless in that the leaves and blossoms arise directly from the root. The pitchers, the leaves, are curved outward to a diameter of one to two inches. The mouth of the pitcher, protected by a flap, has a rolled rim. Located on the flap and rim are numerous nectar secreting glands. These produce a sweetish fluid, the bait, that attracts insects. The inner part of the rim is a slippery surface composed of overlapping cells that have a waxy coating.

Below the slippery zone is a region of long, stiff, downward sloping hairs with many more nectar secreting glands. The bottom portion of the pitcher usually holds a fluid which contains a digestive enzyme. An insect lured by the nectar goes ever farther into the vessel until it looses its grip and falls into the fluid. The downward pointing hairs prevent it from climbing back out, and it drowns. The digestive enzyme, perhaps aided by bacteria, goes to work. The dissolved nutrients are absorbed.

The leaves are strongly veined and are mixtures of reds and greens. They form a rosette with several stages of growth present at any one time. The blossom is supported by a stalk that may be two feet high if the plant is healthy. It also is a reddish color.

115

The round-leaved sundew (Drosera rotundifolia) is probably the one most common to the North Country. This plant is also found in acid peat bogs. I find it right alongside the pitcher plant. The beautiful, translucent green leaves, about a half inch or so across, are covered with tiny, red, hairline tentacles. These tentacles are remarkable in that they secrete a sticky substance that collects in glistening drops at their ends. This gives the plant its name. These tentacles have many capabilities. They produce a digestive enzyme, water when necessary, absorb the digested nutrients and have the ability to move.

An insect, attracted by the glistening little paddle, crawls out and becomes entangled in the glue. Its struggles somehow signal the tentacles to curl over, further entrapping prey. As each tentacle is brought into play, its load of glue is deposited on the insect, and soon the victim is covered with the sticky material and tightly clasped by many tentacles. After several days, when the meal has been digested, the tentacles will unfurl, setting the trap for another meal.

The leaves form a rosette several inches across. The red on green makes a most attractive plant nestled in the sphagnum moss at the edge of the bog. The unspectacular blossom, on a six-inch stalk, may be white, pink or red. While it is structurally less dramatic than the pitcher plant, its actions are more dynamic.

I have kept both as house plants in the past. Feeding was no problem. Bits of hardboiled egg white seemed to be an adequate substitute for the insect prey. Chunks would be dropped into the pitchers of the pitcher plant, while small pieces rubbed over the leaves of the sundew would elicit the clasping reaction. All of the plants thus fed regularly would produce fine blossoms, whereas those left to the occasional fly around the house rarely blossomed at all.

So, while they do not growl or wave menacing arms at every passing animal, they are, nevertheless, carnivors, and we have them in the North Country. While they are not spectacular enough for television, they are still very remarkable in their adaptations for a very specialized way of life. If you should chance to flounder on a quaking bog, take time to inspect its carnivorous residents, examples of the incredible diversity of nature.

116

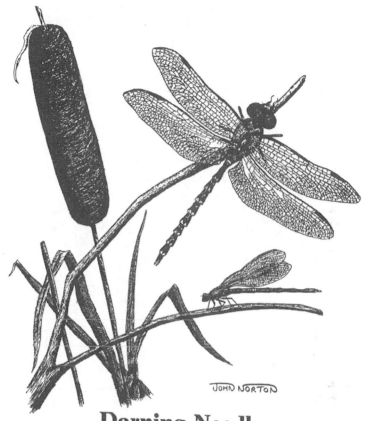

CHAPTER 44

JOHN NORTON

Darning Needle
Fantastic Flyer

"Watch out. Cover your ears. That's a Darning Needle and it will sew them up." That was my first introduction to the dragonfly. As I recall, I tentatively covered my ears and looked at my mother. We were at a picnic, one of the first I remember. She smiled and shook her head to let me know that it wasn't true. I spent much of the day watching this fantastic flying animal and have been an admirer ever since.

There are more than 400 species of dragonflies in North America and nearly 5,000 worldwide. These insects are strictly carnivorous. The young dragonfly, the nymph, is a vicious blood-thirsty predator. The underwater nymph stage varies from species to species. Most species complete their underwater phase in one year. With some it may take five years. The hungry nymph will attack, subdue and consume other insects, but it will, with its lightning fast, clawed lip, capture small fish and tadpoles.

After its required aquatic development, it climbs out on a reed stem, splits its back and out comes the adult version. It is as different from the nymph as night is from day. Large multi-faceted eyes give the head a severe bulging look. The body colors, depending on the species, run the spectrum, red, orange, yellow, green, blue, violet. The body is elongated, the extent again depending on the species.

Organs of Flight

Its wings are large, transparent, glistening, marvelous organs of flight. The dragonfly is the fastest insect in the air. It can hover, fly backward, dart, dive and dip. With a wing beat of over 1600 beats per minute, it can outmaneuver almost anything. Rarely is it the successful object of aerial predation. If there is any doubt about this in your mind, try to catch one with an insect net. Do not attempt this in public, as you are bound to come off second best. The large bulging eyes, so situated as to allow visibility in all directions, plus flying apparatus, will make you look the fool.

The six legs of the dragonfly are located very far forward. They are of little use in walking, but form a basket when in flight that catches insects. As the swift predator moves through the air, the leg basket sweeps up mosquito after mosquito. In some parts of the country the dragon fly goes by the name of Mosquito Hawk.

Mosquito wigglers during the dragonfly's nymph stage, and flying mosquitos during its adult stage, comprise a considerable portion of its dining fare. It is this characteristic alone that makes the darning needle a friend. Enormous numbers of mosquitoes are consumed each day in season. I read recently where a municipality, apprehensive about mosquito control with insecticides, purchased and released thousands of dragonflies.

Some time ago, I was resting after a strenuous stint of hoeing in my garden. The dragonflies were darting back and forth over my head.

I leaned on my hoe handle, quietly following their aerial maneuvering, when one came to a delicate six point landing on the back of my hand, inches from my eyes. I held my breath and faced him head to head.

My first impression was that my companion was sporting a beard. A closer look showed that, protruding from the mouth, were several pairs of small insect wings. My visitor had done most of his dining on the wing. I watched as the beard gradually disappeared. Most of the bodiless wings fell to the back of my hand as he cleaned up after his meal.

Most dragonflies rest with wings horizontal. The damselfly, another of the dragonflies, is a more delicate organism and rests with its wings upright. Mating and courtship take place on the the wing. It is at this time that the pinnacle in aerial acrobatics is reached. Many thousands of eggs are deposited, singly by some species, in clusters by others. Some are scattered on the surface of the water, some placed beneath, some within the tissues of underwater plants.

Unlike many insects, where life comes abruptly to an end after mating and egg laying, the dragonflies survive. They continue, for the rest of the summer, to strain mosquitoes and other insects out of the air. They continue their fantastic aerial maneuverings until the cold of autumn stays their wings. But they have made provision for their successors to appear when spring dawns again. The age-old cycle will repeat.

CHAPTER 45

COMMON MOLE

STAR-NOSED MOLE

JOHN NORTON

Moles
Sublime Marriage of Structure and Function

Some time ago a friend complained to me that moles were eating her tulip bulbs. I tried to explain that moles were classified as carnivores and rarely consumed plant matter.

We inspected her tulip bed. There was no question about moles having been present. I dug up one of the partly eaten tulip bulbs and showed her the teeth marks. The parallel channels made by rodent incisor teeth were quite evident. I tried to convince her that it was mice but she would have none of it. It was not until a year or so later when I dug up a mole and showed her its teeth that she grudgingly acknowledged that perhaps the mole was the secondary cause of her tulip loss.

The moles tunneling in her tulip bed for insects, worms and other animal matter had created fine avenues for the mice. These creatures scurrying along the tunnels feasted wherever a tulip bulb protruded through the walls. The mole had carried considerable unwarranted blame on his shoulders.

There are three moles that one might encounter in the North Country, the common mole, the hairy-tailed mole and the star-nosed mole. The common mole prefers well drained, loose soil in pastures and woods. The Star-nosed mole prefers swamps, mud, even the bottom of streams and ponds. The Hairy mole is somewhere in between.

These mouse-sized and mouse-colored animals are characterized by over developed forelimbs. The forefeet have broadened palms. The limbs are shortened but magnificently muscled.

The animal uses these powerful appendages literally to swim beneath the surface of the ground. It is almost impossible to hold one in your hands. It will force its way out between your fingers with ease.

Mole eyes are tiny and well hidden in the fur. Sometimes they do not even appear through the skin. Vision is limited. The nose is a very well developed organ of touch as well as smell. Both the common and hairy-tailed have noses that are sharply pointed.

Star-Nosed Mole

The star-nosed mole, as the name implies, is something else. This little creature, actually the largest of the three species, has twenty-two, fleshy, pink, finger-like protrusions that grow in a star-like fringe from the tip of its nose. You'll never mistake this animal when you see it. With most mammals the hair has "grain". That is, it tends to grow and lay in one direction. The hair on your dog points toward the rear. Mole hair does not have grain. It can lay in any direction. This is a distinct advantage when traveling in a tight tunnel. When necessary to go in reverse, the hair also reverses direction making for smooth unimpeded movement.

Moles do not hibernate. During the winter months they bore their tunnels beneath the frost line. At this depth they can burrow at a respectable 15 feet an hour. When working near the surface, they can tunnel along at about a foot a minute. Thus a mole does not have to be working your lawn very long to cause considerable havoc.

Such vigorous efforts require large amounts of energy. A mole will consume half its weight each twenty-four hours. Once during the winter we had a mole burrow into a root cellar. The cement walls extended about eight feet below the ground. The mole found a corner hole between the walls and the cement floor and proceeded to give us a pail or two of fresh earth every day or so until we plugged the hole with a wooden peg.

Moles prefer a light loose soil that can easily be worked. Several times during the past I've dug up moles while spading in my garden. The mole vanishing act is an incredible thing to watch. He disappears into the soil right before your eyes.

Many years ago, when I was young, we had a mole in our raspberry patch. Not knowing, at the time, what to do, I started stamping down the ridges only to have them appear the next day. When the ridges began appearing in the lawn next to the raspberries, I obtained a mole trap. This was a device that was supposed to spear the animal as it went along its burrow. It was ineffective. I think I was secretly glad, as I was not too keen on killing the animal.

I really didn't have a serious quarrel with him. Finally someone told me to put mothballs in the tunnels. This worked. I probably over did it as I used a pound of pellets in about 100 square feet, but no new ridges appeared and when after a day I collapsed the tunnels they were no longer rebuilt.

"Why moles?" you ask. We think that everything has to have some value directly for us. We have been led to believe that living things are either "good" or "bad". The science of ecology tells us that living things are interdependent. Taken at its fullest, this means that in some way moles are dependent on us and that we are dependent on them. These dependencies are obscure, to be sure, but they exist. Good or bad has no meaning in the broad scheme of things.

So if a mole disturbs your lawn, use some compassion, some wisdom. Let him exist. Don't obliterate him. Use a pound of mothballs.

CHAPTER 46

Firefly
Magic at Dusk

Some time ago I mentioned fireflies to a friend. He immediately started in telling me how he had played with them as a youth. In late spring and early summer, when the fireflies were at their height, he would go out at dusk and catch a number of the little flashing beacons. These were transferred to a glass tumbler, which sat upside down on the kitchen table. He, and those of his family that were present, would spend the balance of the evening in the darkened room watching the lights flash. At the end of the festivities, the insects were released to be caught again at another time.

I was struck by the enthusiasm that he put into telling the story and even more so as he described, almost exactly, the many summer evenings I had spent those many years ago, doing the same thing. Later I mentioned this to another friend who told me the same tale. Apparently, firefly watching had its aficionados well back before the days of television.

The firefly is a fascinating animal. It, along with quite a few other animals, can produce at will, a bright, cold light. This light is very efficient as far as energy expended is concerned. It has intrigued scientists for centuries. I suspect it intrigues the fireflies also, but for different reasons.

This periodic flashing is a signal, initially, on the part of the male. An interested female then responds with appropriate flashes. The prospective bridegroom or bridegrooms, as it may be, then home in on the receptive bride and a union is consummated. This ingenious and elaborate system is designed to aid mates in finding one another in the darkness of the night. Other insects may use scent, sound or some other means, but the firefly opted for the blinker system.

The fireflies, also called lightning bugs, are neither flies nor bugs, but are a soft shelled beetle belonging to the Lampyridae family. There are a large number of species, each with its own code. The codes may be a series of flashes or may involve a steady beam with a particular flight pattern. Usually the pleading message is executed within a few feet of the ground. The coy female rests on vegetation near the ground. Her reply is also in code. Occasionally, they seem to forget and respond to the wrong code or, in their excitement, respond to any code. However, this idyllic arrangement seems to work, as the firefly has been with us for eons.

Actually, it is not always idyllic. Every good scheme has its usurpers. Every family has its skeleton in its closet. The Lampyridae is no exception. Certain females will respond to the signal of males other than their own species, luring them into a rendezvous. Once within reach, the unsuspecting male is seized and eaten. So much for perfidy and treachery. It exists, at least as we interpret it, throughout nature.

These little beetles range from 5 to 20 mm in length. They are elongated, slender and are usually black or brown, but some are green, even orange. Their bodies are soft, not hard as with most beetles. They are not strong fliers, which is why so many of us were able to catch them. As far as I can discern, they have no ranking as pests. I have read that the firefly larva feed on slugs. If this is so, I place another plus on their side.

Several years ago, my wife and I were taking a late evening walk along a back country dirt road. It was a forested area. We expected to return in the dark. As there was no moon, we took a flashlight with us. Shortly after dusk, a real black night descended and the fireflies came out. The woods around us were awash with tiny pieces of living light. It was magic. The birds had long since finished their twilight serenades. We watched in silence, a ballet with an ever changing choreography.

For some reason, it became necessary to momentarily use our flashlight. I switched the beam on and then off as fast as I could. I did not want to risk turning off the spectacle or to devote time to recover my night vision. As we continued to grope our way along the road, we gradually became aware of a light emanating from my clothing. We checked to find it was coming through the light cloth of my jacket pocket. During the brief period that the light had been on, a male had responded, landed on the flashlight and had been tucked into my pocket. From that hideaway, he continued to signal to the fantastically brilliant lady that had caught his eye.

Here is true magic. The dancing specks of light in the shrubbery that borders your lawn, the myriads of twinkles over a meadow on a soft warm June night, bring an enchantment that only nature, in all her glory, can provide.

About the Author

In 1980 Louis Mihalyi retired from teaching high school science. At one time or another he taught all of the high school sciences but favored Earth Science and Biology. As a retirement project he started writing the "Black River Journal," a weekly column, which has appeared each Saturday ever since in *The Watertown Daily Times*.

Photo by Karen Mihalyi

He graduated from Cornell University in 1943, entered the Army and was commissioned in 1944. He retired from the Army Reserve with the rank of Major in 1981.

A marriage of forty years produced six offspring. Much of his early writings were for the entertainment of these progeny. A series of essays entitled "The Monarch," where he talked with a gigantic oak, helped him impart some of his philosophy and love for nature to these descendants. It was in "The Monarch" that the seeds for the "Black River Journal" were sown.

His home is in the center of a 55 year old 65 acre reforestation with an 1100 foot driveway which he has to plow after winter snows. Behind this forest is a large marsh which occupies much of his warm weather time.

Adjacent to this marsh and reforestation is a 30 acre Christmas tree plantation which he has managed for over twenty-five years.

Always interested in history, he became ever more deeply involved with the Lewis County Historical Society, becoming its president in recent years.

Among his varied interests are: barbershopping, gardening, hiking, hunting, fishing, bird-watching, cross-country skiing, snowshoeing, reading, woodworking, wood carving, recording oral history, beekeeping and conservation activism.

While his nearly 250 "Black River Journal" columns constitute the bulk of his published works, he has contributed to a number of periodicals.

For over three years he has done his writing using a word processor. This has made rewriting and editing a pleasure and has contributed greatly to the joy of writing.

Photo by Ken Wagner

John Norton

Although he had been drawing since the first day he could hold a crayon, John Norton didn't begin to seriously develop his skill as a nature artist until he began to do the illustrations for "Black River Journal." John never had formal art training; instead, he developed his technique by studying the work of other illustrators.

John was raised in Constableville, N.Y. and attended the South Lewis Central School system where he had Louis Mihalyi as a biology teacher. In 1982 he graduated from Syracuse University with a B.S. in biology. From there he went on to Clemson University in South Carolina where he is now working toward his master's degree in the Aquatic Sciences under Dr. James E. Schindler. Presently John is a laboratory instructor for Introductory Biology and is the editorial cartoonist for the University newspaper. John plans to pursue a career in the natural sciences that will permit him to use and further develop his artistic talents.